Stories of Children Learning to Read

Susan O'Leary

TWG™

The Wright Group • Bothell, Washington

© 1997 Susan O'Leary
© 1997 Wright Group Publishing, Inc.

Library of Congress Cataloging-in-Publication Data

O'Leary, Susan, 1950–
     5 kids: stories of children learning to read / Susan O'Leary.
       p.   cm.
     Includes bibliographical references (p.).
      1. Reading—Remedial teaching—Case studies. 2. Reading
(Primary)—Case studies. 3. First grade (Education)—Case studies.
I. Title.
LB1050.5.O54 1997
372.4'3—dc20   96-33357
                                                    CIP

Cover design and illustrations by Dave Cap

The Wright Group
19201 120th Avenue NE
Bothell, WA 98011

Printed in the United States of America

10 9 8 7 6 5 4 3 2 1

ISBN 0-7802-8059-8

For my Madison family
Jim, Nate, Nora, and Tom,
and my parents
Ginger and Gar O'Leary

Contents

Acknowledgments   ix

Introduction   1

Reading Recovery: An Overview   9

Fortune
A Homeless Girl   39

Nicholas
A Writer's Son   65

Kareem
From the Chicago Projects   85

Nkauj Hli
Daughter of Refugees   133

Rebekka
The Failing Poet   161

Conclusion   201

Bibliography   207

Acknowledgments

I would like to thank my son Tom for being born. This book was written before his birth and after it, a few hours a day, a few days a week, in the time I had off from teaching because of his birth. As the mother of a young child, I am tremendously fortunate to know that when Tom was in child care with Sister Theresa Panther and Sister Marie Therese Kluethe, he was well loved. This book would not have been written without their presence in Tom's life.

Early readers Susan Herndon, Jane Mitchell, Steve Benson, Nora O'Leary-Roseberry, Maureen Ruzicka, Dirk Dickson, Barbara Keresty, Mary Jones, Mary Thompson, and Sister Donna Kucenski all helped me believe that this book would be published.

My friend Charlene Zabawski is a writer's dream editor. Charlene has one of the quickest, most cohesive minds I've ever known. She knew when my chapters needed honing; she knew when they didn't. This book would not be what it is without her.

It has been a pleasure to work with Stephanie Fowler, my editor at The Wright Group. She has asked questions I would have preferred she didn't ask and made me come up with good responses to them. Her sense of organization complemented well what I wanted to say. I thank Dave Cap for foregrounding the children in his book design.

For help along the way, I thank Chuck Curtis.

Clearly, Marie Clay's writing has been fundamental to my book. My intention is that my stories of children whose lives her theories have changed will bring a new audience to her writing.

I teach at one of the best schools in the nation, Franklin School in Madison, Wisconsin. I would like to thank all of the staff for their commitment to children and their sense of humor, which make going to work a vocation, not a job, for me: Margie Allen, Mary Beck, Mary Bingham, Becky Briles, Winifred Brown, Jean Cree, Susan Daugherty, Paula Devroy, Dave DuRose, Rosanne Ehrlich, Pat Farino, Christine Flores, Kathy Frederickson, Connie Hay, Sally Helgeson, Bee Her, Susan Herndon, Nancy Hodapp, Connie Hood, Myra Hoye, Steve Kailin, Dee Keleny, Emmy Kennedy, Tracey Kennedy, Nina Knapp, Joan Kruse, Annete Kuehl, Mary Kuemmerlein, Andrea Leffingwell, Lynn Legler, Lavone Libert, Bettine Lipman, Nicole Lopez, Andy Mayhall, Patty McCormick, Mac McVey, Rita Miller, Sue Moberly, Cheryl Morrison-Weeks, Paul Natvig, Dee Nicolai, Joan Panepinto, Patcharin Peyasantiwong, Carole Pingel, Mary Powell, Carol Quam, Julie Riewe, Sheryl Rowe, Barb Rubin, Maureen Ruzicka, Chris Shelton, Marilyn Smith, Susan Smith, Ginny Stanek, Carol Tiemann, Pat Vandenberg, Dan Wood, Dick Yelczyn, and Joan Zechman.

Marlys Sloup and Dale Wortley, my Teacher Leaders in Reading Recovery, are deeply dedicated to teaching and to the well-being of children. They are superb teachers, and I have learned more than I can say from them. Whatever I didn't learn, whatever failings this book has, are to be put clearly at my feet, not theirs. Madison is extremely lucky to have these two women living and working—overworking—here.

Elena Chavez-Mueller has a similar commitment to the English as a Second Language children in the Madison Metropolitan School District. Her advocating again and again for our children helps the ESL teachers concentrate on teaching.

The writings and example of Thích Nhât Hanh and Chân Không have had a tremendous influence on my teaching. I thank them for their work in the world.

And I thank the others who have been true teachers in my life: Norbert Blei at Lyons Township High School; Peter Brooks at Yale University; Douglas Kelly at the University of Wisconsin–Madison; the six-year-olds who teach me now.

To return to the beginning, I thank my family. My husband, Jim Roseberry, fostered my desire to write when it meant he then had less time to himself. My older children, Nate and Nora, spent a summer and a school year with my not answering them quickly, with my saying, when they wanted something, "I'm writing now," and they continued to think my writing was important.

And for my roots, I thank my mother and father, Virginia Earle O'Leary and Garner William O'Leary. My mother, through her example and her voice, taught me to love to read. My father taught me to stand up for what I believe in, at times to his dismay.

My great-great grandfather, Jerimiah O'Leary, was a hedgerow teacher in Kilrush, Ireland. When it was illegal to teach the Irish to read, upon threat of imprisonment or death, he was secretly teaching the written word and its beauty. I thank him and his wife, Johanna McCurdy O'Leary, for the love of written meaning they passed on to me.

5Kids

Introduction

Five Kids is about five first-grade children, all from the bottom of their class, learning to read in Reading Recovery®. It is equally about why teachers teach and who children are.

I love my work, and I expect that shows in the book. I have great respect for my students and learn from them daily. Six-year-olds see the world with a freshness and belief that adults have forgotten. They are comfortable in silence, if it suits them. They can be immediately amazed by seeing something new and exclaim over what they have found. Their freshness, comfort, and amazement are profound skills to bring to learning, but for various reasons the children I work with have not been able to apply who they are and what they know to learning to read. With Reading Recovery, they learn how to read and how to succeed in school.

I wrote this book for three reasons. First, I wanted to introduce Reading Recovery to a wider audience and felt I could best do that by writing in lay terms and telling the stories of individual children. Dame Marie Clay developed Reading Recovery in New Zealand in the 1970s. It is an intensive, one-on-one accelerative reading program that takes most

1

children from the bottom of their first-grade class to the middle of their class—where they stay as they progress in school—in only one semester of instruction.

Clay's theory of reading is firmly based on psycholinguistics. It draws on all aspects of written language—semantics, syntax, and graphophonics—in teaching children to read. The children are taught to think about meaning as they read, to draw on their unconscious knowledge of language structure, and to develop the ability to visually analyze words in text. From the beginning, the children learn to integrate the different cues from these aspects of language as they read.

Reading Recovery teachers are trained to closely observe children every day to see what they know and to build on the child's knowledge as a strength. We take that strength and teach to it in order to accelerate the child quickly away from failure. Since traditionally children at the bottom of the class are taught and seen in terms of what they *don't* know, I find Clay's model a great relief. I have learned more about teaching from Clay's work than from anyone else I have read in years of teaching.

I hope that administrators, school board members, teachers, and parents will read *Five Kids* and, if they are in a district without Reading Recovery, will work to bring it to their school. An address to contact for more information on Reading Recovery can be found at the end of the bibliography.

My second reason for writing *Five Kids* was to show who the children are that the Reading Recovery program reaches. There are wonderful, creative children from every sector of society at the bottom of each first-grade class, and they don't deserve to fail. In Reading Recovery, I have taught professors' children and children whose parents get behind on their rent, children whose parents have read to them every night since they were born and children whose parents are illiterate. Anyone can have a child who can't read.

The five children in this book give a good sense of the range of students we teach. I tell stories of Fortune, a spirited homeless girl who was at Franklin School just long enough to learn to read; Kareem, a troubled boy from a Chicago ghetto whose experience was so limited he didn't know the meanings of the words *tomato* and *lettuce* in the first grade; Nicholas, the withdrawn, unsure son of a regional writer who was alternately trying to mask and accept his failure; Nkauj Hli, a Southeast Asian refugee girl who was afraid to ask to learn in a second language; and Rebekka, an abstract, poetic girl who had poverty, dialect, and lack of experience against her. I hope if we see how capable and vastly different our failing children are, we will want to do more for them.

Lastly, I wanted to show what it is like to teach Reading Recovery as part of a school community. Reading Recovery is taught at my school, Franklin School, because the staff has a commitment to teaching all children to their potential and to helping them feel that they belong here.

Franklin School is a desegregation K–2 primary school in Madison, Wisconsin. It was created in 1984 when two proximate city neighborhood schools, Franklin School and Randall School, were paired. (Randall School is now for third- through fifth-grade students.) The Randall neighborhood, where my family lives, is predominantly well educated and professional. The Franklin neighborhood is an old, solidly middle-class neighborhood reaching into pockets of real poverty. Right between the two neighborhoods is Bayview, an area of low-income housing where most of the residents are Southeast Asian refugees. The school reflects the varied city landscape. The poorest of the poor, children who go home to apartments with no furniture or to the Salvation Army Homeless Shelter, attend school with blue-collar children, the mayor's children, and children of university professors.

Franklin School works because it has a tremendously dedicated teaching staff and the support of parents and volunteers, many of whom have made a commitment to mentor at-risk kids. It's inspiring just to walk through the library of the school, because you'll usually see three different tables with adults talking closely with the child they come once a week to mentor. Franklin has also worked because up until now we have had close to sufficient resources to teach our children well.

The other books on Reading Recovery don't foreground schools as community because they are rightfully academic books in which Reading Recovery is the whole and the schools where the research is done are the part. *Five Kids* is written from the perspective of a teacher in a remarkable school where Reading Recovery is the part and the school is the whole. At Franklin, we feel a responsibility to teach children not only academics but also how to feel a part of and get along with others in society. That belief, that it matters to us as a society that all children feel they belong, is also a part of my teaching in Reading Recovery.

Part and whole, whole and part.

I have been an English as a Second Language teacher at Franklin since 1988 and have taught both ESL and Reading Recovery there since 1990. I was in the second Madison

Reading Recovery training class; two of the stories in this book are from that year.

I became a Reading Recovery teacher for both educational and intellectual reasons. Like any teacher of first-graders, I simply could not help some children enough; there were some children who, as hard as they tried and I tried, could not learn to read. It is commonly accepted that ESL students will read below grade level, and before I became a Reading Recovery teacher, most of mine did. But the logic of ESL children being below average has always seemed to me askew. Shouldn't we assume that a child who at an early age has learned the skills to navigate two languages and often two cultures will do *better* than average in school? Doesn't this point to promise rather than failure? I thought that as a Reading Recovery teacher I would also learn how to better teach my ESL students, and I was right. I did.

At the same time, at a theoretical level, what I knew of Clay's work was very exciting to me. My doctoral dissertation, written years before I knew I would teach children, was on the semiotics of allegory in a medieval romance—it was arcane, rarefied abstraction that I loved. In the process of writing it, I studied structural and poststructural linguistics, Russian Formalist theory, and semiotics. Vladimir Propp, Ferdinand de Saussure, Walter Benjamin, Roman Jacobson, Noam Chomsky, Michel Foucault, A. J. Greimas, and Umberto Eco all shaped my view of language, representation, society, and meaning. Traces of their influence are there in how I teach Reading Recovery now.

I have always loved words, and reading is one of my greatest pleasures. This meant that in college I built a major around reading nineteenth-century novels and learning languages. In graduate school I dived into the relationship between words and things. And now as a teacher, I help failing children find their way to reading. These are all parts of the same cloth.

Five Kids is organized as a series of stories about children I have taught. I have altered details of the children's lives and changed their names. I have also, with regret, not credited their classroom teachers by name to help protect the children's anonymity.

I call these chapters "stories" rather than case studies, because stories are how we traditionally convey deeper meaning in society. They mean something, and they mean something else. My stories tell how children at the bottom of their class learn to read; they tell who many of the children are in the United States at the close of the century. They tell of a teacher's relationship with children, working from seeing who they are and expecting them to do their best.

These stories were written in my first years as a Reading Recovery teacher, when Clay's *Early Detection of Reading Difficulties* was the standard text for Reading Recovery teachers. Some aspects of how I teach are different now—I teach more visual analysis than before; I am more aware of the importance of fluency in reading; and in the writing portion of the lesson, I now more genuinely have the story come from the child's own experience. But each of these are refinements on what I learned in those first powerful years of being a Reading Recovery teacher. What matters here is the children with the method, not the details.

The stories are preceded by an overview chapter on Reading Recovery. This chapter is aimed at people unfamiliar with Reading Recovery. If you want to skip straight to the stories, please do so, and then use the overview as a reference as you read, if you like.

A friend of mine, Kathy Bonus, recently said, "I'm glad I teach in the schools, because if I didn't, I might forget that life is chaos." She's right, as any teacher knows. An unfortunate part of modern American life is that most of us who are well educated can lead lives separated from people in need and then forget what hardship does to you. Many children, and not just poor children, live in the midst of tremendous uncertainty, struggle, and change. They have no control over this, and they show amazing equanimity and perseverance in living difficult lives. I recognize that the children I have taught have made my life deeper and that they have taught me thankfulness and a little humility.

Before becoming a Reading Recovery teacher, I could help faltering children make some progress, but the ones who needed the most I could do the least for. Now I have learned to observe children to find their strengths and to construct my teaching so that I am always teaching them the most powerful next thing they need to learn in order to succeed. I feel it's a rare gift to have the opportunity to teach like this.

Reading Recovery
An Overview

This chapter is meant as an introduction to Reading Recovery. Please feel free to skip it if you are familiar with Reading Recovery or if you are more interested in the stories and want to use this chapter as a reference as you read.

I have tried to present an overview of Clay's theory and its implications in lay terms. For a deeper understanding of the process that led to the development of Reading Recovery, I refer the reader especially to Clay's books *Reading Recovery: A Guidebook for Teachers in Training* and *Becoming Literate: The Construction of Inner Control.*

Introduction

Reading Recovery is an intensive, one-on-one reading program for first-graders from the bottom of their class. It was developed by Marie Clay in New Zealand in the 1970s. The goal of Reading Recovery is to, in just one semester, take children from the bottom of their class to firmly in the middle of their class—with the skills to remain there—through daily, individual thirty-minute lessons specifically tailored to each child. We reach that goal with most of the children we teach.*

A full program in Reading Recovery consists of the Observation Survey, two weeks of "Roaming Around the Known" sessions, and about sixty formal lessons. (Sixty is the norm, but the number varies from student to student: Nicholas needed only twenty-one lessons, Kareem had over one hundred. Students like Kareem, who need more than sixty lessons, usually continue in the program.)

Reading Recovery, when fully implemented, can change the feel of a school. If the children at the bottom of the class can read, the classroom teacher teaches a very different class. Higher-level concepts can be introduced for everyone. Discipline problems that occur when a child is failing often disappear once the child feels that she is a successful part of

---

*Almost thirteen thousand students were served nationally in 1992–1993 in Reading Recovery. Of those students who had sixty or more lessons, the national average of students who successfully read at a first-grade level at the end of first grade was between 83 percent and 87 percent (see *Partners in Learning: Teachers and Children in Reading Recovery* by Carol A. Lyons, Gay Su Pinnell, and Diane E. Deford [New York: Teachers College, Columbia University, 1993]).

Dale Wortley and Marlys Sloup, my Teacher Leaders in Reading Recovery, have been tracking the results of Madison, Wisconsin, Reading Recovery students on the Wisconsin Statewide Third-Grade Reading Test since 1995. On this test, students must read and answer comprehension questions about several passages. Using all Reading Recovery students as a base, including those who did not discontinue the program, they found that roughly 70 percent (73 percent in 1994; 68 percent in 1995) of the former Reading Recovery students scored at average or above on the statewide test. Two years after one semester of intervention, the students who had started out as the lowest in the school now tested as average or above on an independent state reading test.

the class. The whole school benefits from Reading Recovery being available to first-graders who need it.

But to me, the most significant impact of Reading Recovery is its effect on children's lives, one child at a time.

Acceleration and Building on Strengths

A fundamental principle of Reading Recovery is that its one-on-one instruction is meant to accelerate the child's learning so that she can catch up to the middle of the class. One-on-one instruction is valuable in itself for almost any child and will help her learning and self-confidence. But Reading Recovery instruction is focused, accelerative, psycholinguistically based instruction in the strategies that good readers use—each day tailored to the specific child's needs.

The strategies introduced always build on the child's strengths because another principle of Reading Recovery is that every child *has* strengths—even if those strengths are as slight as knowing just some letters of the alphabet, some concepts about books, and how to write her name in capital letters. We learn best building on what we know and feeling that we know it well. Reading Recovery students are given repeated opportunities to read and write easily so that the ease, not confusion or uncertainty, becomes a framework for new learning.

Because the child feels successful and because the teacher each day carefully chooses what book she will introduce and what strategies she will focus on to most successfully accelerate each one, the child learns quickly.

Observation

Another essential element of Reading Recovery is that our teaching comes from our daily observation of the child, observation that takes place as we teach. (The paper we write our lesson plans on is even structured with mostly empty areas so that we can easily take notes on the child's strengths and needs during the lesson.) This child-centered, organic approach allows our teaching to be much more powerful than it could be if we had a predetermined path we assumed every child would follow in learning to read. The daily return to observation reminds us to see each child fresh each day and to remember that in seeing him closely we are learning from him what he needs most to be taught.

Becoming a Reading Recovery Teacher

Reading Recovery teachers go through intensive weekly training in their first year and continue in training each subsequent year they teach.

In our initial year of training, we take part in weekly seminars taught by Reading Recovery Teacher Leaders, where we learn the processes and implications of Clay's profound method and theory of reading acquisition. At the same time, we are applying what we are learning in the daily teaching of four students. Each seminar session begins with the Reading Recovery teachers-in-training observing a peer teach a student behind a one-way mirror. While they are observing their peer teach, the Teacher Leader poses questions to guide them in thinking about how to structure the lesson to best accelerate the student's learning. In this first year, the Teacher Leader also regularly visits us at school to observe us teach and then discuss with us our teaching and the students' needs in learning to read.

In subsequent years of training (our training is never complete), we attend four in-services a year, we are observed teaching at our school by our Teacher Leader, and at times we visit each other to observe and discuss lessons with children who are difficult to accelerate. This continued contact allows teachers to reflect on their own and their colleagues' teaching, and to reflect on their deepening understanding of the process of reading as they teach.

Reading Recovery is a program that teachers feel passionate about. Many of the Reading Recovery teachers were already the best reading teachers in their school when they began training. Learning and applying Clay's theory, they were suddenly able to teach reading to children whom they hadn't been able to reach before. As a Reading Recovery teacher, you feel a commitment to this program because you have never seen anything so profoundly change a child's life and potential in school.

The Reading Recovery Program

Observation Summary

Each year a Reading Recovery teacher begins by observing the children she will work with perform different tasks. The teacher checks the child's knowledge of the alphabet, the words the child can write in ten minutes, the child's understanding of concepts about print, his ability to identify words in isolation, his ability to write a dictated sentence, and his ability to read elementary text. The teacher then writes a detailed Observation Summary of the child's skills, gleaning as much as she can about the child's strengths and problems with reading and writing from closely analyzing the records of what she has seen the child do. The Observation Summary guides her initial teaching; it is also referred to when a child hits a particular difficulty in his program.

Roaming Around the Known

"Roaming Around the Known" is the name given to the first two weeks that the child spends one-on-one reading with the Reading Recovery teacher. The half-hour sessions in these weeks are not formal lessons; instead they give the child repeated opportunities to work with what he knows in reading and writing and to become fluent and flexible with that knowledge. During this period, the teacher and the student are immersed in reading and writing at a level where the child will be successful.

In Roaming, the teacher doesn't teach. Instead she helps the child see what he can already do. He can perhaps read very simple text; he can sort letters of the alphabet to find the ones he is sure of; he can (with the teacher) write stories using words he already knows. (This writing vocabulary may at first be as minimal as his name and the word *Mom*.)

In Roaming, the teacher and child return again and again to the same books, and the child, finding more each time in the book, becomes more confident about her ability to read. Often, in the unpressured structure of Roaming, the child will demonstrate more knowledge than she was able to show initially. She will know the sound of more letters; she will correct an error she made; she will become confident writing a few simple words. Formal lessons are intense and demand concentrated attention from the child. The two weeks of Roaming help to build the child's perception of herself as a reader and writer and to bring all she does know to an automatic level so that she will be successful once lessons start.

In these two weeks the child and teacher also form a relationship that will be the basis for the more rigorous daily lessons. Children at the bottom of the class often are not used to feeling that someone has seen them do something well. But because Roaming is based on what the child knows, he can repeatedly succeed and do things easily. With success, he comes to expect the teacher's confidence in him.

For the teacher, having the luxury of concentrating on one child without interruption allows her to develop a different relationship with the child than would be possible in the classroom. By focusing only on that child for an entire half hour, she can become as aware as possible of the child's strengths. A tremendous trust can build between a teacher who is truly observing and a child who feels she is being seen succeeding. With that trust and awareness, accelerated learning begins.

The Reading Recovery Lesson

After the two weeks of Roaming, individual lessons begin. Each lesson follows the same structure: the child rereads familiar books, then reads the book introduced the day before for the Running Record (discussed below). The teacher makes teaching points about the book used for the Running Record and then teaches the child some elements of word analysis. After this, the child is asked to write a little story, usually one sentence long. Finally, the teacher introduces and the child reads the new book, which will be the basis of the Running Record in the next lesson.

Within this structure, the teacher develops different lessons each day for each child. The lessons always draw on that individual child's strengths, make learning easy, and lay the groundwork for the strategies the child needs to learn next. And again, each day's lesson is built on the teacher's observation of the child.

Familiar Rereading

The child begins each lesson rereading books she is already comfortable reading. This helps her to consciously start the lesson feeling like a reader. In reading these books fluently, she draws on meaning, structural, and visual strategies in order to read. This use of several strategies in fluent reading primes her for the Running Record.

The Running Record

During the Running Record (when the teacher records "on the run" what the child says when reading), the child independently reads the book he has read only once before—at the end of the previous day's lesson. For the Running Record, the teacher acts as a neutral observer, telling the child a word only when the child is truly stuck. This part of the lesson helps the child become used to problem solving on text—a critical skill for struggling students—and gain confidence in using new reading strategies. It is when the teacher can truly observe *how* the child is reading text as a whole.

The Running Record the teacher takes each day is a quick, clear transcript of all attempts the child makes when reading. On it the teacher records every word read correctly with a check mark and codes all repetitions, rerunning starts (returns to an earlier part of the text), substitutions, phonetic attempts at words, insertions, deletions, pauses the child makes, appeals by the child to the teacher, self-corrections, and words supplied by the teacher. After the child has read, the teacher quickly makes one or two teaching points about the child's reading of that book. The points are chosen according to what the teacher thinks will help that individual child on that day most quickly accelerate in reading.

After the lesson is over and the child has gone, the teacher analyzes each error and each self-correction to see if the child was using meaning, the structure of language, or attention to the printed letters and words on the page in each error or self-correction, and if these cues were used in an integrated way. The teacher also writes a short analysis of how the child in general used cues and strategies in reading that day. These daily analyses help us see what cues the child relies on and what strategies need to be taught. As they read, fluent readers draw on all three elements of written language: meaning, structure, and the visual representation of words. If the child is overrelying on one, we ask strategic questions to draw her attention to using the others.

The Running Record also gives a record of the child's accuracy in reading that day's text. We aim instructionally for children to read daily at 90 percent or better accuracy. Obviously, children don't always read at this level of accuracy, but if they range consistently below, that is a good indication that the child is reading text that is too difficult. Consistent accuracy in the high 90s or at 100 percent means that the child is ready to move on to harder text.

Reinforcing Letter Knowledge and Word Analysis

After the Running Record part of the lesson, the teacher spends a few moments securing letter knowledge and letter-sound correlation for children who are not yet sure of these visual and symbolic aspects of reading. The children are given repeated opportunities to identify letters and match those that are not yet securely known using magnetic letters. They may also be shown repeated examples of words that start with a particular letter in little letter books.

Children are also taught with magnetic letters how to bring high-frequency words to writing fluency. Perhaps most important, they are taught how to use analogies to figure out and learn words. They learn that *man* is like *ran* and *can;* that they can build a knowledge of *in, it,* and *if* from securely knowing the word *is;* and that knowing *is* can also extend to learning *his* and *him.* If the students can in early lessons learn the words *in, it,* and *if* because they know *is,* they are learning a powerful strategic lesson: I know this because it is like something else I know. This strategy of association then becomes a means of learning many other words and parts of words.

Writing the Sentence

The child now writes a sentence, with correct spelling, as independently as possible. Often the sentence has to do with the story just read during the Running Record—what it was about, what was his favorite part—but it can also come from the child's life. The child writes every sound he hears; the teacher fills in all other letters. As the lessons progress, the child generally passes through several stages of awareness of writing.

In the beginning, many of our students don't know how to write all the letters of the alphabet. Some may be able to associate only a few sounds with letters. Early lessons focus on increasing awareness of letters and sounds and of words. Here children are taught to form and write letters that appear in the sentence they generated, to listen for sounds in words, to leave spaces between words as they write, and to practice high-frequency words until they can write them fluently and easily. As the lessons progress, children learn to hear more sounds in words and eventually to hear the sounds in order. They learn to make associations between words. For example, we tell them that if you can write *book,* you can write *cook;* if you can write *can,* you can write *man.* They are shown these analogies over and over until they understand the idea of generating one word from another. They learn to write words as parts, clapping to hear syllables and gaining mastery over chunks like *-ing, -ed,* and *-er.* The attention to visual detail, sound, and analogy in their writing transfers to their reading and helps them read increasingly difficult words and sentences.

The child writes the day's sentence on a page of the writing book, with teacher help whenever necessary to fill in sounds or letters so that the words are spelled correctly. This interactive writing, where the teacher assists the child in writing at the edge of the child's capabilities, helps accelerate the child's writing in several ways. Interactive writing is not a solitary process. Young writers working alone (just like older ones) can often get stuck, not knowing what to do next. They erase their paper until there is a hole in it and then worry about the hole. They sharpen a pencil that has already been sharpened. They sit, unable to remember what they are writing about because they aren't sure how to form a letter, and in the process of thinking hard about what *b* looks like or how *the* is spelled, they forget the sentence they were going to write. With a teacher sitting right next to them, they are repeatedly brought back to the focus they need. They daily learn the rhythm of writing well.

The teacher, at the appropriate level for the child, also models the process of hearing sounds in words. If the child is having difficulty hearing beginning consonants, the teacher will model listening for them, saying, for example, *"Book.* I hear a *b* at the beginning of *book."* The teacher, not the child, then writes the letter *b* in the child's sentence because the teacher is the one who heard the sound. The child writes the letters that she herself hears.

This process of listening together for sounds also helps the child hear more sounds in words than she would on her own. When the teacher models hearing the first *n* in *banana,* the child may then be able to hear the second *n* independently. Similarly, being able to hear the consonant framework of a word (all of the consonant sounds in a word) is often a first step for the child to consistently hear vowel sounds in words. The teacher's daily modeling of listening for sounds and then writing them is a crucial part of the Reading Recovery child's quick acceleration in writing.

The correct spelling used in this interactive writing also gives the child expanded opportunities to look at words as they appear in books. (In inventive spelling, also called temporary or developmental spelling, children write words the best they can, and incorrect spelling is accepted. This is an excellent primary-grade classroom technique for developing both phonological awareness and an appreciation of the pleasure of getting your thoughts down on paper. In Reading Recovery, because the teacher is working daily one-on-one with an individual child, the words can all be spelled correctly because the teacher quickly fills in the needed letters as she and the child work on words.) The child sees words correctly written and correctly spaced as she writes them in her writing book. She will see them again in reassembling her cut-up sentence in her Reading Recovery lesson and practicing with it at home that night (see page 23).

In this daily writing with her teacher, the child uses two pages each day—a writing page and a practice page. On the practice page above the page on which the child is writing the sentence, the child practices whatever elements of writing will most accelerate her learning to read and write. It may be working on difficult letter formation. It may be writing high-frequency words several times that her teacher has chosen to focus on from her sentence. This process is called "taking a word to fluency." In learning to write common words easily, the child begins to experience fluency in writing and develops a base for monitoring words in reading. When a word is solidly fluent in writing, the child is more likely to recognize it in text.

On the practice page the child also uses Elkonin boxes to help her practice listening for and writing sounds of words. Elkonin boxes, developed by the Russian psychologist D. B. Elkonin, are boxes drawn on a page to help the child see a space for a sound as he or she says it. If, for example, the child is listening for sounds in the word *milk,* the teacher draws four connected boxes on the practice page as follows:

She then puts a counter under each box and prompts the child to push a counter into the appropriate box as the child slowly says each sound of the word. When a child hears a sound, he says, for example, "I hear an *m,*" and then locates the box he hears it in. When he has correctly identified a sound and where it goes, he writes it in the box. The teacher fills in letters that are not voiced and sounds the child does not hear.

Early on, the child learns to stretch the word out slowly, saying one continuous word.

Physically moving counters as they say sounds has the same power for developing children's spelling that physically pointing to words as they read does for developing children's ability to see words in reading. With the practice of Elkonin boxes, children come to hear sounds in order and to hear all or most of the sounds in words. The teacher then switches from using sound boxes (one box for each sound) to letter boxes (one box for each letter) to facilitate the connection between writing and the conventional spelling children will find in books. The child's ability to hear sounds in writing is reinforced by the teacher as a corollary to reading. Eventually this ability transfers in their reading to an ability to see letters and then quickly expect the sounds in order that go with those letters.

For the end of the writing time, the teacher copies the student's sentence onto a strip of paper and then cuts the sentence into parts for the student to put back together. In early lessons the sentence may be cut so that the student sees groups of words. As lessons progress, individual words may be cut apart so the child can see and become aware of common word parts, for example, *-ook, -at, -an,* and so on. Each time the sentence is cut to meet the particular child's needs at that point in the program. In searching for the right word or part of a word, the student learns to monitor and look at words closely. After the student has practiced the cut-up sentence, it is put in an envelope, with the full sentence written on the front of it, for the child to take home and practice that night.

Introducing the New Book

The lesson ends with the introduction of a new book. In preparing this day's lesson the day before, the teacher has thought about the lesson just finished—how fluently the child read at the beginning, read the Running Record book, wrote her sentence, and read the new book. Unless the child was struggling, the teacher would then choose a new book that was slightly more difficult than the previous lesson's new book to help the child become secure in a known strategy or to develop a new one.

The teacher introduces this new book to the child by going through it page by page, discussing the pictures and story, and highlighting one or two words she expects may be difficult for the child. The child is told the general idea of the book, not as a crutch, but so that early on she is learning to read for meaning.

After the teacher introduces the book, the child then makes a first attempt at it. When the child has difficulty with a word or phrase, the teacher asks questions that help the child develop strategies for reading. In beginning lessons, these prompts may be as basic as teaching the child to point to every word read so that the child really becomes used to looking at print. Intermediate questions ask the child to become aware of thinking about meaning ("Does that make sense?"), language structure ("Could we say it that way?") and the visual elements of reading ("What would you expect at the beginning of *star?* Does it look right?"). By the end of the program, the questions direct the child to call on strategies himself. If the child is stuck on a word, the teacher might simply say, "What could you do to figure that word out?"

The books used in Reading Recovery are chosen from reading series like The Story Box® (The Wright Group) and from trade books. The children are taught with books from several publishers so that they will see a variety of book sizes, print types, and illustrations, with language that is not confined to a controlled vocabulary. I now have about six hundred books in my Reading Recovery collection. (Ideally, I should have even more.) I add to my books every year so that each day when I choose a book for a child I have the best chance of finding the right book for accelerating the child's learning the next day.

All Reading Recovery books have been assigned reading levels from one to twenty. These quickly tell a Reading Recovery teacher the difficulty of the book. Level one is simplest; level twenty, the most difficult. (Level twenty is not used with most children but may be used at the end of the first-grade year with some children in Reading Recovery.)

Most children do not pass through all text reading levels in the Reading Recovery program—this would be contrary to the philosophy of starting where the child is and quickly accelerating her learning. At the beginning of first grade, our students will typically be reading at level one, two, or three. The second-round children, taken halfway through first grade, may start at level two or three or even at level five, six, or seven. Most children progress through levels in order, but some will skip levels if the Reading

Recovery teacher sees they are ready to read more difficult text.

Reading Recovery reading levels correspond generally to the following traditional levels in basal series:

Basal Level	Reading Recovery Levels
Readiness	Text reading levels 1–2
Preprimer One	Text reading levels 3–4
Preprimer Two	Text reading levels 5–6
Preprimer Three	Text reading levels 7–8
Primer	Text reading levels 9–12
Grade One	Text reading levels 13–17
Grade Two	Text reading levels 18–20

Levels one to four generally have one to three lines of text on a page with clear spacing between the words. The story is told in a simple, repetitive pattern, and the illustrations on each page clearly demonstrate the meaning of the words on the page. These are short books with as few as twelve or fourteen words and a maximum of fifty or sixty words.

Levels five and six may have up to four lines of text on a page. The repeated language pattern is somewhat more complex. The spacing between words is not necessarily as wide as in the earlier levels. There is often a stronger story line with a clear beginning and end. These books can range up to about one hundred words.

Levels seven and eight are now not necessarily patterned. The pictures still support the text on the page, but a longer, more complicated story is told. These books can range up to about 150 words.

The first eight levels generally have been written with oral language structure. Levels nine through twelve now may blend oral and written language structures. Folktales like "The Gingerbread Boy" and "The Lion's Tail" are examples of books written at these levels. These books are generally 100 to 150 words long. Shorter books at these levels do not have a predictable pattern.

Levels thirteen through seventeen are often longer stories with increasingly difficult language structure, more literary language, and more varied vocabulary. "The Three Little Pigs" is an example of a book at these levels.

Levels eighteen through twenty can range into first chapter books like the Frog and Toad series or familiar trade books like the Clifford series. They have varied text, sometimes with double meanings, and the pictures no longer clearly support the text.

The Three Elements of Written Language: Meaning, Structure, and Visual Representation

Clay's theory of reading draws on all aspects of written language in teaching children to read: semantics (meaning), syntax (structure), and graphophonics (visual representation of sound). The children are taught to think about meaning as they read, to draw on their unconscious knowledge of language structure, and to develop the ability to visually analyze words in text. From the beginning, the children learn to integrate the different cues from these aspects of language as they read.

Meaning Cues

Meaning is the first level of language that is brought to reading. It is what the story or the page or the sentence is about, and it is the most important level of the text. It is the element of language that in linguistics is called *semantics.*

In the early books children read, meaning is summed up by the picture on the page: "A dog. A cat. A ball. A box." Children who understand word patterns in books (all of the phrases above include the word *A* plus a noun) and look at pictures in order can read a simple book without looking at the words, paying attention primarily to meaning and structure. That is why some children can start out seeming to do very well in reading and then get lost. They don't learn the crucial phase of "attending to print," or learning to look at words.

As children progress to more sophisticated books, they have to pay closer attention to the words on the page (visual cues) in order to read correctly. One picture now supports more than one sentence, and the children can't read the book from just pictures and pattern.

But what they read still has to make sense. And for this they draw on meaning. They still use the pictures to frame the meaning of what they read, but now they also draw meaning from their sense of what stories are about and from their expectation of what will happen next.

At an elegant, dialectical level, we bring meaning *to* reading in order to draw meaning *from* reading: what we already know helps us predict and confirm what the next part we read is about. The new meaning, understood and synthesized with what is already known, is in turn brought to the next section of text and so on. Reading Recovery students are not taught at this level of abstraction, but they are taught to understand the meaning of the text as a whole (the teacher, until the final lessons, always introduces the book by summarizing it with a few sentences) and as parts (the teacher and student then look through the book discussing each page before the student reads). They are also taught fundamentally that it matters that what they read makes sense. We read books to find meaning.

Structural Cues

Structure, or *syntax,* is the second level of language that is brought to reading. It is the order of words in a sentence. All speakers of a language bring an unconscious knowledge of the structure of that language to speaking and reading it. Native speakers of English know that adjectives come before nouns, that articles come before adjectives, and that subject nouns usually precede verbs in sentences. The words *The girl saw the dog* make sense because of their structure. But *The the saw dog girl* does not make sense because the word order is not meaningful in English.

We draw heavily on our knowledge of structure while reading. We are able to predict what comes next in a sentence in part because we know what kind of word to expect. Children draw on structure when learning to read by using this unconscious structural prediction. They also draw on structure in using simple patterns in early books ("My nose. My mouth. My eyes. My face.") and more complex patterns in intermediate books ("Lazy Mary, will you get up? Will you, will you, will you get up? Lazy Mary, will you get up? Will you get up today?").

Children who speak in dialect, or speak English as a second language, cannot always draw on the structure of language found in books as easily as native speakers of standard English can because they bring different expectations for grammatical rules to their reading. For these children, structure can be a barrier to reading. Hmong children often drop the final _s_ on verbs and plural nouns when they read because their native language doesn't show tense or plural with an added final consonant. Children who speak Black English have different rules for conjugating verbs than those used in standard English. These children will commonly read present tense for past tense in books because that is how the words would be spoken in Black English. They are predicting language structure just as children who speak standard English do, but they are predicting it according to different rules of grammar. Structure is a powerful element of language, which we draw on constantly when predicting and reading. It is also the element of which we are generally the least aware.

Visual Cues

Visual cues are the third element of written language that is brought to reading. In linguistics, the use of visual cues is called _graphophonics_, or the written (graph) representation of sounds (phonemes). Thus visual cues, at what is usually an unconscious level for fluent readers, combine sound and form. They are the written words (which the eye can take in as isolated letters, parts of words, whole words, and series of words), the spaces between them, the punctuation marks we use in writing, and the symbolic relationship between letters and sounds.

As children learn to read in English, they learn to follow visual cues with their eyes moving in a line from left to right. They learn that after finishing a line they come back again to the left and read the next line below it, or if there are no more words, they go to the next page to the right and start again at the top. They learn to see words within these lines because they know how to read and write isolated words like their name, names of family members or friends, or the word *stop* from stop signs. They begin to develop a sense that words are letters in a certain order. Children also use visual cues to make sure that they read one word out loud for each word in the book. That is, to match four words on a page, they read "I have a puppy" instead of "I like puppies." This matching is called one-to-one correspondence.

Children's initial awareness of text focuses on visual cues at the level of *grapheme,* or signs on a page. Children at first may or may not be aware that certain individual signs (i.e., letters) represent certain sounds. But in learning to read, children need to learn to recognize and identify the letters of the alphabet and to put one or more sounds with each letter, for example, the *s* and *k* sound for *c,* or the hard and soft sounds for *g*. They then use this letter-sound knowledge to begin to monitor that the words they are saying are actually the words in the book: That word is *Dad* instead of *Father* because it starts with a *D,* not an *F*.

As children become more focused on looking at words, they usually become aware of the first letter of the word, the last letter of the word, the consonant framework of the word, parts of words like *-an* or *-in,* and vowels. Having achieved this level of visual processing, most children start to learn to read across words, seeing the letters or parts of words in order. They use their awareness of letter-sound relationships to then say sound after sound and part after part in the correct order and to decipher unknown words.

In Reading Recovery, long before we ask children to read across entire words, we have been developing the child's ability to do this in the writing part of the lesson. Each day they slowly say words and use Elkonin boxes to push counters into boxes as they listen for the sounds they say. The important link between writing and reading helps them learn to transfer their ability to hear sounds in words they know to using sounds to figure out words they don't know.

Other Reading Strategies

Attending to Print, Monitoring, Searching, Cross-Checking, and Self-Correcting

A foundation of Clay's method is to make absolutely certain that struggling children are really looking at each word as they read. Clay calls this behavior "attending to print." It is a crucial goal of instruction in the early levels of books, and its importance cannot be overemphasized. The child must pay attention to the words on the page.

Early lessons focus on getting the child to attend to print in part through the kinesthetic skill of pointing to each word as it is read. In this way the child learns to see and read what is there. Once the child has become attached to print, the teacher focuses on drawing this ability to see what is on the page into the skills of monitoring.

Monitoring is an awareness of when you are right and when you are wrong. It is a crucial aspect of learning to read that many children who are struggling with reading fail to get under control. Monitoring, in its most elementary form, is simply learning to look at the words on the page and to follow them one by one in reading. In early lessons we teach the children, over and over, to point to every word as they read. Most children don't need to do this, but pointing is a tremendous help to the struggling beginning reader because the physical act of pointing keeps them focused on the page, on the line, on the word.

After children learn to point to and see every word and to be aware of some visual features (e.g., noticing the first letter of a word, seeing high-frequency words as a whole) or when they show evidence of stopping when they recognize they have made an error, we then teach them to become more sophisticated in their monitoring, to search for what is right.

Searching teaches children how to look more closely at words and how to think strategically about text. Children can be aware a word is wrong without knowing what to do to correct their error. Searching is the process the child uses to find the correct answer.

Children who don't succeed in school often are not flexible in approaching a problem. They will attempt one strategy and give up, or they will repeat the same unsuccessful strategy. The students at the top of the class have learned to be confident in trying one approach, and if that doesn't work, then trying another and another. The flexibility that Reading Recovery children learn in approaching problems is one basis for their quick acceleration.

When a child stops at a word and knows it is wrong, we teach her to choose the most powerful question for the situation: "Does it make sense?" (meaning); "Can we say it that way?" (structure); "Does it look right?" or "Are those the letters I would expect to see?" (visual cues). When the child begins to apply these strategic questions on her own as she reads (and they may be neither voiced nor consciously used), she is *cross-checking* elements from one system of language against another. For example, saying "in-over-under" for *on* is an attempt to use structure to arrive at the right word; each time the child realizes that the attempt does not look visually right. When cross-checking results in reading the word correctly, the child has self-corrected.

The child will *self-correct* early on in his program simply by noticing that he has read too many or not enough words for the page. As he progresses into more difficult text, his self-correction will be based in a variety of ways on monitoring, searching, and cross-checking. We note and teach self-correction from the very first lessons; it is a powerful strategy used by successful readers and, circling back to the beginning, a clear way to teach the child to attend to print.

Fluency

Fluency is not a strategy but an essential element of good reading. Struggling readers rarely get a chance to practice reading fluently and with expression because once they have struggled through a book or a story, they don't see it again. Instead they are given another book or story to struggle through. Without the opportunity to return frequently to known books (and to have the number of known books grow), they don't get practice in using higher-level reading skills and orchestrating strategies for fluent reading. Ironically, when children having difficulty with reading are pushed along at a pace that is too difficult, they are kept from being good readers because they don't get practice in reading well.

In Reading Recovery, children start each lesson reading well by reading familiar books. Each night they take home familiar books to practice with their family members. In the lesson, the teacher also models what fluent reading sounds like, giving the child a chance to read fluently after her. That way the child understands that fluency is a part of being a good reader. What the teacher draws attention to is what the child will learn.

Rerunning Start

What Clay calls a "rerunning start" is a powerful integrated reading behavior. Some of us were taught to teach children to skip difficult words and read ahead in order to figure out the difficult word by seeing what came after it. In observing successful young readers, Clay found that though they might tell you they skip hard words and read ahead (parroting back what they have been taught), they actually do the opposite. They start the sentence over in a new approach to the difficult word. In making this rerunning start, children are able not only to draw on meaning as they read but also to unconsciously use their knowledge of the structure of language to predict what the difficult word is. When a child, having taken a rerunning start, gets her mouth ready to say the difficult word as she gets to it, she is able to draw on meaning, structure, and the visual configuration of words all at once in predicting the word. The rerunning start is one of the most powerful skills a teacher can teach a beginning reader.

Conclusion

First grade is a crucial year for children because it is the year when most children learn to read. Children know how they are reading and how their classmates are reading. In many ways they find their place for themselves and their expectations of themselves by comparing themselves with their classmates. You can do away with reading groups; you can call reading groups Zebras, Giraffes, and Lions. But almost any child by the end of first grade will be able to tell you where they fit in class as a reader, who reads better than they do, and who doesn't read as well. And by the end of first grade, the children at the bottom of the class are not only struggling in reading but also often becoming defeated about who they are. No matter what we do to cover the difference and downplay its importance, if they have any smarts, they've learned they are dumb.

Struggling children can have very different needs. One year I tried to imagine how I would teach my four Reading Recovery students together as a reading group. Caitlin needed to learn to really look at words on a page and carefully follow them with her eyes; she also needed to learn a variety of reading strategies that would help her get around the blocks she had in remembering. Chava needed repeated instruction in letters and sounds because in many cases he couldn't make the correlation. Joshua, who was *only* focused on sounds of letters as he read, needed to learn to keep thinking about the general meaning of the story and to expect words to be there because they would make sense. Then he would be able to use his well-developed phonics skills to check to see if the word looked like what he expected. Caruna needed more experience with words and descriptions of concepts. She also needed experience visually analyzing words she didn't know in order to learn to bring together new meaning with its unknown visual representation.

If these four students with such different difficulties in learning to read were clumped together in one reading group, even with the finest teacher, they would each make some progress, but I doubt any of them would ever get out of the bottom group. Instead, they would continue to fall further and further behind their peers. In Reading Recovery they are given a chance to accelerate and catch up to their average peers. They are given a chance to succeed.

Fortune
A Homeless Girl

Fortune arrived at school a day out of the homeless shelter, a month after school started. Her mother, a rough, brassy, opinionated woman, had Fortune and her two sisters in tow, all of whom she was registering for first grade. Fortune and her twin sister, Anastasia, were just ten months younger than the older girl, Spirit.

I was there filing papers when they hit the office like a whirlwind. The mother was talking loudly and making her expectations clear about the kind of education her children should get, as she randomly and sporadically disciplined them. Fortune's mother spoke regularly with asides—whatever she was doing she would comment on. In this her introduction to the school, she explained that the twins looked so much alike that she couldn't always tell them apart unless she looked closely. She had just yelled at Anastasia instead of Fortune by mistake—"Just goes to show."

Anastasia and Fortune, meanwhile, were flying around the office, talking a mile a minute while they fought and ignored their mother. Anastasia's and Fortune's long blond hair curled all over and flew around with them.

Spirit's blond hair was straight as a yardstick; it made a solemn line down her back as she stood quietly watching her mother. Spirit was more aware of the impression they were creating on the school and seemed to want half a chance.

That was the first I knew of Fortune. After they left the office, I rolled my eyes and told the school secretary that whoever got those kids in class had my sympathy. Two weeks later, because the child I had been working with suddenly moved, I was working with Fortune.

Fortune and Anastasia had settled in to their separate first-grade rooms, cased the joint, and started stealing what hadn't been nailed down twice. (Spirit, in a third first grade, was still being quiet and serious.) But in Fortune's and Anastasia's rooms, suddenly the students couldn't play board games because the game pieces were missing. Pencils, erasers, markers, and learning materials disappeared. When Fortune's teacher told the mother at a conference that the girls might be taking things, she said, "Oh, yeah, I wondered where all that was coming from." She never sent any of it back, though.

Fortune was random, impulsive, and unable to sit still for any amount of time or pay much attention to what she was doing. She was smart, and you could tell thoughts were racing through her head, that it was her imagination that kept distracting her. Though she could blow up or get hurt easily, she was also eager and positive, quite sure the world was welcoming and that she had a rightful place in it. Despite my first impression of her, I quickly respected this optimism in a child who, at barely six, had lived in four different states and been homeless.

There was a cartoonlike explosiveness and quickness to the way she would say things. Not just quickness, but intensity too, as if she were trying to fit everything she could into each frame. And just as she was intense, she was oblivious to her effect on things and to the larger picture around her. She focused on whatever mattered to her immediately, and whatever it was, that was her world.

All of these qualities—her intelligence, her imagination, her inability to stay with a task—came through in the diagnostic materials I gave Fortune. Fortune was clearly a smart kid— that is, if you looked at her in isolation, not as she presented herself in the classroom. There she rarely worked and rarely concentrated long enough to understand things. She was quickly falling behind other first-graders in reading.

One of the texts we ask children to read when we are deciding which children to work with has the clear pattern, *So can I.* We prime the children with the pattern in the book twice before we ask them to read it alone. Fortune read the pattern right the first two times, switched it to "I can, too" the third time, and just looked at me sweetly, saying nothing, for the final two pages. Her response was a good indication that Fortune was not paying attention to the pattern or even looking at the page.

We also ask children to write as many words as they can in ten minutes. Fortune wrote eight: *Fortune, Anastasia, Spirit, Mom, Dad, red, is,* and *Papermate.* (She had seen the brand name on my pencil and methodically copied it.) A few months into first grade, then, Fortune could write only two words aside from the names in her family: *is* and *red,* her favorite color.

Because first-grade children can often read words they can't write, we give them a list of high-frequency words to attempt. Fortune sat silent when I showed her the words and didn't try any.

But the tasks Fortune performed also showed she had strengths we could work from in teaching her to read. She could identify all but four of the uppercase and lowercase letters in the alphabet. The letters she was confused by were visually similar: *b/d, h/n, l/i,* and *q/p.*

She could also hear and then write thirteen out of thirty-seven sounds in a sentence I dictated to her. This score was rather high for a child at the bottom of the class.

Finally, she understood many concepts about books and print. She knew where to start on a page and which direction to read in. She knew that we read the left page before the right, that capital and lowercase letters are analogous. She knew the difference between the first and last letters of a word, and most important, she knew the difference between a word and a letter. (Many children at the bottom of the class do not understand this difference. In fact, the difference is a difficult symbolic concept.) All these invisible elements of reading can be huge barriers to children. Fortune's understanding of the many symbolic levels of reading made me feel confident that although her skills were limited and scattered, we had a solid, unusually abstract base to start with. Fortune and I, together, would teach her to read.

Before formal Reading Recovery lessons begin, the teacher and student spend two weeks doing informal work called "Roaming Around the Known" (see pages 14-15). The child is asked to do only what she has already shown she can do. Children at the bottom of the class are often unsure of and doubtful about their skills. By giving them many opportunities to do well what they can do, an enormous pressure is lifted from them. They start to think they are capable rather than incapable. Succeeding in reading, they even initiate new strategies or go back to old strategies they had given up on.

Roaming is a time for the teacher and student to get to know each other and for the child to gain confidence. In our first Roaming session I read books to Fortune that we and then she would read again and again in the next two weeks. Because she could write her name and the word *is,* and could readily hear many sounds in words, we played an interactive writing game in which Fortune wrote "Fortune is" on the board and then finished the sentence however she liked. Fortune wrote the sounds she heard, and I supplied the rest: "Fortune is playing." "Fortune is a bike rider." (The underlining shows what Fortune wrote; see pages 19-23 on the interactive writing process.)

She liked the book *Where's Spot?* by Eric Hill, so together we started a book called "Where's Fortune?" On each page we put a self-adhesive note that represented a place where Fortune might hide. On the first day we wrote together: "Is she under the bed?" We then lifted the flap, and she wrote under it,

"No!" I was surprised that Fortune was familiar with exclamation marks. It meant that, at least sporadically, she was paying attention to the detail of print.

At the end of the first Roaming session and every succeeding one, I read a very easy book to Fortune (one with as few as fourteen words) and then suggested she read it to me. She always could, and by the end of the ten sessions she had a repertoire of ten books she felt confident reading.

In the first session I modeled pointing word by word as I read. I didn't ask Fortune to do it but waited until she initiated it herself. As we reread a book I had just read, Fortune began pointing to the words in the book. This one-to-one matching, a practice often discouraged in schools ("Read with your lips, not your finger"), can be a crucial skill for students who are struggling with reading. For a distracted student like Fortune, it is a quick, simple way to get her to notice word after word on a page. By the end of Roaming, with no pressure on her, Fortune was not only pointing to words as she read but also monitoring to see that they looked basically right. She would go back and start a sentence over if things didn't match.

On the second day, when I read her Helen Oxenbury's *We're Going on a Bear Hunt*, she pointed to the word *mud* and said, "That's *mud*." I think she figured the word out because of the context and because she knew the sound *m* makes. Not feeling the pressure to read or perform, Fortune was starting to really look at books.

By the sixth day we finished her "Where's Fortune?" book. In the fourth and fifth sessions she wrote *the* on her own, but in the sixth session she couldn't write it. Acquiring and then losing words is common for children who are learning to read (and is a reason why "taking a word to fluency" [see page 22] is part of the Reading Recovery program).

By the seventh session Fortune was one-to-one matching well and reading with expression. She went back and corrected incorrect pointing by recognizing that she was pointing to the word *the* but saying another word. Pointing, correcting, and reading with expression were all skills she initiated on her own.

With the pressure off and the daily half hour spent immersed in reading and writing, Fortune was even starting to think about the first letters of words. She would volunteer, "That begins with an *s.*" "*Put* starts with a *p.*" "*Now* starts with an *n.*" For children struggling to learn to read, this spontaneous learning won't usually just happen on its own. The child needs a knowledgeable teacher to create the right setting and then sit back. But with a relaxed atmosphere and the teacher observing, not directly teaching, the child can gain tremendous confidence and attempt more and more. The teacher, meanwhile, by listening to the child's responses, learns much more about what the child actually knows about reading than diagnostic testing could show.

By the end of our Roaming sessions, Fortune regularly self-corrected many errors. She monitored to see that what she read looked right and would start a sentence again if she was off on her one-to-one matching. She could confidently write and read eight new words: *a, and, go, I, no, the, to,* and *yes.*

She was ready now for the rigor of the lessons. But though Fortune had picked up many skills in Roaming, the formal lessons soon showed that she hadn't secured them all. She was still pointing, but not necessarily under words. I took that as my main focus in the initial lessons, and she soon was back on track. Before Roaming, Fortune couldn't read a level one book successfully (see pages 25–27 on book levels). By her fourth Reading Recovery lesson she was in level four, reading at 100 percent accuracy. But she didn't always read that well. Fortune's earlier randomness showed in her daily Running Record scores. Until the eighth week of lessons they bounced around—93 percent, 75 percent, 83 percent, 96 percent. I had to learn to look at her reading with a day as a whole and with several days as a whole to understand how she was putting things together, what she was indeed learning.

I loved how Fortune's name fit her. She seemed like an icon of herself—happenstance, luck, fate. Though her first six years had been rough and chaotic, she was quite a happy and open child. She bulldozed through life, sure of her place in it. Somehow it fit with Fortune's sporadic good and bad luck that, although she had just been homeless, she was now getting premier one-on-one reading instruction.

Fortune was a whirlwind, her life was a whirlwind, and her place in the world, her sense of physically belonging, mattered considerably to her. She wanted to make sure I knew exactly where her locker was and what was in it, because it was clearly hers. She showed me her name on the outside, formalizing her claim on it. She told me the contents of her backpack as she rummaged through it, looking for the books she usually forgot to bring back.

As we walked through the gym to the reading room, Fortune told me about her family's new apartment. It bugged her that Anastasia was always getting into her things, although

I suspected she was equally into Anastasia's. She described corners of rooms and what she did in them, how she made them her own.

Fortune was especially proud of her mother. A week after they had moved into their apartment and started school at Franklin, her mother had managed to get their bus stop moved to a safer place to cross. We were impressed when we heard this at school. And it fit with what I knew of her mother from that first office visit and several phone calls we had had. Her attention—and it was intense—seemed always focused on what outraged her. She lived in the moment, not long-term.

But Reading Recovery didn't outrage her, and she was intense about that, too. She told me that she herself had had a hard time learning to read. She appreciated this opportunity for Fortune and wanted to know when Anastasia could start. Anastasia hadn't been chosen for the program because she was doing better than Fortune in reading.

Fortune seemed like her mother in how random she was in learning and how intensely she lived each moment. I studied this part of her, for to pull Fortune in and to help her accelerate in reading, I had to understand as well as possible how she learned, what she brought to reading and what she left out.

Children learning to read do not draw on only one linguistic feature, that is, meaning, structure, or visual cues. But they will often *rely* primarily on one of those elements. Fortune's early errors in Reading Recovery were generally meaning based. This pattern was compatible with her intensity and randomness. She would read "lamb" for *sheep*, "Bobby" for *David*. This was actually a good sign—if I could just get her to look more carefully at the book, she would succeed, because she had already learned that what you read should make sense. Not all children are aware of this.

But Fortune had gaps in her learning. She didn't know, for instance, what a rhyme was. Though she could write *is,* she didn't understand at first that it sounded like *his.* Rhyme is an abstract concept that most children just intrinsically understand. It is a phonemic element that in reading we grasp graphophonically, or visually. Because it is at once obvious and abstract, it can be hard to teach to children who don't understand it.

I knew I would need to focus on rhyme right away because early readers use rhyme in multiple ways to build fluency in reading. It can help them master more difficult text. For example, they use rhyme to predict what the long word at the end of the sentence will be: "I just read *mouse,* so this must be *house."* They use it to help commit short texts to memory. This allows children to practice reading at the level of expression and fluency, not word by word. It is for these reasons that so many children feel their first real sense of accomplishment in reading Dr. Seuss books.

Rhyme also helps children understand an essential analogy in reading and writing: words with similar chunks will probably sound alike and be written alike. At an early level we teach them, "If you can write *cat,* you can write *bat.*" "You can read *book.* What do you think this word is? *Look.*" If children can understand this concept of generating one word from another, they can later transfer it to reading more difficult texts. They can quickly take a new word apart by syllable or by chunk and read across it without losing the meaning of the sentence: *bull-do-zer, stamp-ing, bum-ble-bee.*

Acquiring a knowledge of morphemic chunks such as *-ing, -ed,* and *-s* also helps children become accustomed to unconsciously cross-checking their structural knowledge of English with the visual elements they see on the page. If the child knows the story is being told in the past, he will know that "ed" sounds right at the end of a verb and "s" sounds wrong. A six-year-old, of course, won't be able to tell you why she knows this, but if she is a native standard English speaker, she *will* know it. Reading Recovery students aren't taught generative linguistics, but they are taught, at a six-year-old level, how to draw on their knowledge of what language sounds like and when it is coherent. We tell them, "Make sure that what you read looks right and makes sense," and this continual prompting directs them to checking their skills.

All of which leads back to Fortune's not understanding rhyme. I needed a place to start with her so that she could learn to generate words. And to do that, she had to learn to hear what a rhyme is.

What helped me in this was that Fortune was constantly excited by new things she learned. Knowledge and the world were simply amazing to her. The drawback was that new thoughts seemed to constantly bombard her and take her mind quickly somewhere else. She would be reading a book, writing a sentence, or putting a word together with magnetic letters, and suddenly she would look up at me and say, "Yeah but..." "Yeah but" was one word to her, and the beginning of any digression or new wonder. "Yeahbut, did you know that my mom brought a *kitten* home from the *bar* last night for us? And she said we could *keep* it?" She underlined words as she spoke, giving emphasis to what mattered most to her. "Yeahbut, did you know that Carrie was really *mean* to me in class today? She said my *socks* didn't match, and they *do*. Look." And she would start taking her shoes off to show me that her socks were exactly the same, though inside out. "Yeahbut, the *moon* goes around the *earth,* it really does. How does it do that?" Fortune would turn in her chair and be ready for a long digression, speaking quickly. Each time I would have to bring her back to what we were working on.

In a classroom with twenty to thirty kids, it is almost impossible to keep bringing students like Fortune back to task. Their imagination and excitement about learning becomes an impediment to learning. But in the tight structure of one-on-one teaching in Reading Recovery, children like Fortune are continually guided back to what they need to know. After repeatedly being shown how to put words together and take them apart with magnetic letters ("Make *my*. Now make *by*." "Make *cat*. Now change it to *sat*. To *bat*.") and being encouraged to listen to how they were the same and different, Fortune did learn the concept of rhyme, and it became a strong base for her to build on.

Fortune slowly began focusing more closely (though not terribly closely) on words as she read. Whereas at first her substitutions had been things like "lamb" for *sheep,* she now was reading "I see" for *It sees*, "roar" for *roars*, "mean" for *my*.

The time we spend analyzing Running Records and the child's other daily work allows Reading Recovery teachers to see that these kinds of errors are progress. Fortune was finally paying close attention to the first letter of each word she read. The written text had become more meaningful and much more important to her than it was before she started in Reading Recovery, when she was simply inventing text. Fortune now knew to look at words on a page. It also meant that she began to struggle in her reading as the texts got longer.

As Fortune began to substitute visually similar words for the words on the page, she lost meaning. This caused her to flounder, frustrated, until she sat with fists tensely clenched in her lap, saying nothing. As soon as she knew something was wrong, Fortune pounced on herself, telling herself she was a failure. Her tense, scruffy face would become very internal, revealing her resignation. She was very proud; pride was one of her best defenses, and it enabled her to fight off the other children's jibes. But she couldn't feel proud now, lost in confusing words. She couldn't look at me; she couldn't try.

I would try to pull her back with questions about the text, and Fortune would look up forlornly and say, "Doe-e [another of Fortune's expressions, a grace note and down a half step], I can't do this." I had to find the right balance to help her learn. If I supported her too much, she wouldn't learn how to solve problems independently. If I didn't give her enough support, she would remain convinced she was a failure. I asked her questions to help her figure out words rather than just giving her the words. I made sure she knew I thought she was smart. And with that trust and expectation, she would start again, hands still tight in her lap, now going uphill.

Fortune knew I cared about her, and that knowledge, too, helped her learn to read. I valued her imagination, the part of her that continually hurt her in the classroom because she couldn't pay attention. She would take my hand and skip when we went to read, chattering away. My concentration on Fortune helped her learn to concentrate on school.

In her tenth lesson one of Fortune's errors showed she was now starting to look at more than the first letter when trying to figure a word out. She read, trying several times, "I-I'b-I'b-I'b-I'b" for *I'd*. Many children have a hard time sorting out the difference between *b* and *d* in first grade, so I wasn't concerned about that. What I saw was that Fortune was both attempting to read the whole word and realizing that what she said wasn't a word. She persevered; she tried four times to read the word correctly. She read it slowly and each time knew it was wrong. She didn't give up, and she knew it didn't make sense. This was real progress. When we had first started reading together, she had blithely ignored her errors. Now she was aware when she made them.

The next few weeks of our working together were the hardest ones for Fortune. She had to learn to integrate meaning and visual reading skills and not rely solely on one or the other. Fortune was being challenged beyond what she thought she could do, and she showed a six-year-old's dignity and courage in facing it daily.

Often at the beginning of the lesson, when we were taking a word to fluency (now words like *said, here,* the chunk *-ing*), she would keep rattling off thoughts: "Yeahbut, I don't like *Anna,* she's *mean* to me." "Yeahbut, did you know that today we've got *music?* I *like* music." I would tell her to write her word again, and with that as her latest thought, Fortune would quickly comply and then sit down.

In our first lessons, Fortune read little books fifteen to forty words long. Now the books usually had fifty to one hundred words, and they had more plot than short books allowed. Fortune had to read at a new level of meaning, one page continuing rather than essentially echoing another. Responding to more extended meaning and having acquired better visual skills, she was starting to more consistently self-correct. By the middle of December, she often had a self-correction for every two errors she made. But she also had days when she lapsed back into inventing text, reading "Here they are the was" for *Said Nick, "Here they are!"* The only clue that Fortune was looking at the text was when she read "the" for *they*. But then she totally lost meaning.

Her Running Record scores kept jumping around: 89 percent, 95 percent, 75 percent, 90 percent. The low scores usually came after a difficult night at home. Fortune wasn't getting regular sleep because her father now had a night job as a cook and her mother often went to a bar, leaving the girls with an older brother. Six-year-olds can't function well in school without enough sleep. However, I kept taking her to harder books because I saw that she was learning more difficult skills all the time.

And Christmas was coming, as Fortune continually reminded me. She now often wore a red velvet Christmas dress to school, and she would show it off for me when I picked her up for her lesson.

Her daily writing turned to Christmas: "I like Santa because he gives me presents." (The underlining shows the letters Fortune knew; I filled in the end of *presents* for her because we were running out of time.) Fortune's sentence showed that she was now aware of silent *e*, could discriminate short *i*, heard sounds in order in words (an essential advanced skill for readers and writers to develop) and heard beginning, medial, and ending consonants. All this was done without her filling out long pages in reading workbooks.

Two days before winter vacation Fortune proudly brought me a present that to her was astonishingly beautiful. It was a picture of a Hummel-like figurine of two children that her mother had let her rip out of a *Woman's Day*. Fortune continued to hold onto it after she had given it to me, not entirely sure she wanted to give it up. But it was also clear she wanted me to have this wonderful picture because I listened to her dailiness and cared for her. I gave Fortune a book, of course.

It was now winter vacation, and Fortune had had twenty lessons. In her first lesson she had read *If You Meet a Dragon...* (The Wright Group), a pattern book with strong picture cues to guide her. It essentially repeats a pattern:

Tickle his back.
Tickle his nose.
Tickle his legs.
Tickle his toes.
Tickle his tail.
Tickle his chin...

The last day before vacation she read *Bruno's Birthday* by Marcia Vaughn, a book with a much more complex narrative and no patterned sentences:

Today is Bruno's birthday.
He has a cake with four candles.
For his birthday, Bruno is getting a brush and a ball.
Bruno's friends are coming to his party.
"Happy Birthday, Bruno!"

Fortune had learned to monitor text and to read for meaning. She was working on new skills such as generating words. Just as she had earlier struggled with the concept of rhyme, she was now having a problem with these new skills. But Fortune was no longer so far below her classmates. She was gaining confidence and gaining a seriousness in class.

Fortune came back from winter vacation and told us she was moving in two weeks. Her family was going to get a house with a big yard, and she would go to school on the other side of town. The school she would be going to had no Reading Recovery program, so now I suddenly had only two weeks to teach Fortune everything I could.

Fortune wasn't far enough along in reading skills to maintain what she knew and to continue to progress rapidly without Reading Recovery lessons. She was finally consistently reading the words, but she didn't have the skills to make sure they made sense. I was now trying both to teach her enough that she could successfully graduate from Reading Recovery, and to teach her whatever I could for reading survival in case she wasn't at Franklin long enough to graduate.

So we continued to work on mid-level Reading Recovery skills: generating words, attending to first and last letters and known parts of words, working to make sure that one system of reading skills—meaning, structural, and visual—correlated with another.

As Fortune got better at visual analysis, her errors became more slight: *mushrooms* for *mushroom; carrots* for *carrot*. But they showed she was still not carefully monitoring the end of words.

Fortune's writing skills were always ahead of her reading skills; they were in part her window into reading. "I'm moving next month," she wrote, hearing all but two difficult sounds *(e* and *x)*. Then two days later: "I'm not moving until March." (Again, for the sake of time, I completed the last word for her.) It was only January. I now had some time to work with.

Fortune was a low-achieving, poverty-level child who had been homeless, and she could now write like this halfway through first grade. She heard sounds in words well and in order, but she wasn't yet transferring that ability to her reading.

In her Reading Recovery research Clay found that some children, like Fortune, could analyze sounds in spoken words and use that skill in writing but not apply it easily to reading. Others could analyze signs (letters) in written words, but couldn't transfer what they knew about reading to writing. Clay's research clarified that the first skill involves an auditory, sound-sequence analysis. (As beginning writers, children use this skill when they say words slowly to themselves.) The second involves a visual, letter-sequence analysis. They are different but almost converging skills, but writing is not reading, and proficiency in one does not always transfer to the other, especially for early readers.

When children learn to apply what they know about writing to reading and what they know about reading to writing, their skills in reading generally accelerate. They are learning to use the higher-level skill of analogy—how writing is like reading or reading is like writing—to solve problems. Children who have trouble learning to read often don't do this.

I needed to show Fortune how to transfer her remarkable writing skills to reading. She could hear sounds well, but she couldn't analyze letters in text as easily. To learn this skill, she needed to learn to monitor text closely as she read so that what she said made sense and matched the text. It meant she would have to learn to cross-check visual cues with meaning and structural cues by reading what she would expect to be there (drawing on her knowledge of the book she was reading and of how the structure of English sounds) as she checked to see if she was right. This is the skill of prediction, grounded in syntax and semantics, that fluent adult readers employ all the time as they read.

To help Fortune integrate these skills as she read, I taught her to "get your mouth ready" for a word coming up. This simple phrase of Clay's is a kind of magic for some children, especially children who learn more kinesthetically, that turns print into words flowing from words, helping children read more fluently, as they prepare *physically* for one word right after another. This phrase also connects, at an unconscious level, the meaning, structural, and visual cues. Because it links systems, it brings a new pace to reading as meaning drives what children see.

At each new level she reached in reading, Fortune's visual skills always lagged behind her other skills. But she was a quick learner with a quick memory. She kept building a knowledge of words that gave her more fluency in her reading. By lesson thirty-three she was reading "where-what" for *what,* "does-do" for *do,* and "what-who" for *who.* Each first attempt was visually similar to the correct word; each correction was for meaning.

I started to realize that Fortune was wearing a lot of new clothes to school—not only Fortune but also Anastasia and Spirit. Buying clothes for three girls takes a good deal of money, and I worried about what was going on in the family. Was their mother using rent money to dress the girls so well? Life in Fortune's home continued to seem pretty chaotic. Fortune was supposed to be reading a Reading Recovery book at home every night to reinforce what we had done that day. If she took a book home, it was immediately lost. Fortune was sure it was Spirit's or Anastasia's fault. I would call the mother, she would really clean, and every two months or so, the books would come back in a clump.

The stories about how big the yard at their new home would be grew. This was a castle that Fortune was getting a chance to imagine, a real house where she would live perhaps forever. The family drove out one Sunday to see the girls' new school. The field around the school was so large that Fortune thought they were in the country. On our daily walks to my room, she would describe what she imagined the inside of the house would look like. She would have her own room, and Anastasia wouldn't always be in her things. Everything would be clean. It was going to be beautiful. That imaginary house carried Fortune through many days. I think it's the nicest place she ever lived.

The sentences she wrote were usually about the books we read, but now and again they told about her life, the life of a poor child: "I go to the hospital when I'm sick." She heard sounds in order as she wrote the three syllables hos-pi-tal, and she heard most vowels now. She didn't know the security of a family doctor. Medicine and illness meant hospital emergency rooms to her.

As well as she was doing, Fortune would have days when she crashed. She would suddenly be vulnerable and lose her self-confidence. She sat defeated and refused to try until I gave her the hard word to keep her going.

Now Valentine's Day was coming. Fortune geared up for holidays, excited by the possibility in them. She started wearing her red Christmas dress again, explaining that this dress could be for both days. She told me early on that they were going to make a cake at home for Valentine's Day, with lots of red hearts. She would bring pink cookies to school to pass out to everyone. Then, as Valentine's Day got closer, she varied her litany. Her dad was gone, but they would have a special Valentine's celebration with him when he got back. Every day she told me her dad was gone but that he would be back.

I called her home, one of my regular calls about missing books, and Fortune's mother told me they were going to be evicted. She had spent the rent money on car insurance; she had to drive, didn't she? She didn't know where her husband was or when he'd be back.

I called the school district social worker who works with homeless children and their families to see if he could do anything. I wanted to buy Fortune time. He told me why Fortune's father was gone. He had been following mail carriers on the east side of town, watching for boxes of new checks to be delivered. He would open the box, take out the bottom check (so no one would miss it), and write himself some money. He had written quite a few checks before the police found out who he was. He made it out of town right ahead of them.

What this meant for Fortune was that she could disappear at any time if her father came back quickly for the family. Again I was up against a wall in teaching her to read. Her life was set out for her to go from crisis to crisis. I wanted to give her this one thing to rely on—knowing how to read— before I lost her.

In her last month with me she had only one difficult day with reading—the day after Valentine's Day. With her earlier excitement about Valentine's Day with her whole family, her confusion on February 15 told me more about her life than about her reading ability. After lesson forty-five Fortune was predicting using meaning and structure, paying close attention to the visual elements of words, and self-correcting errors. She was reading stories like "The Three Little Pigs" and "The Great Big Enormous Turnip."

Fortune told me at the beginning of March that they were moving back to Maine because her dad was in jail there. "He got caught *drinking* and driving. I don't like it when he does *that*—alcohol's a *drug*. One time he told us to wait in the *car* 'cause he was going into the *store* to get a *Coke*, but he came out with a *beer*. I don't *like* that.

"I *hope* we don't move back to the place with *cockroaches*. I *hate* cockroaches."

Fortune's dream house with the big yard and her own bedroom was gone for her now. She had spent weeks imagining it and preparing to live in it. Now she spoke differently about where she would be living; she quickly accepted the new, lesser reality. She didn't chatter. She was serious and frank, her voice was lower, and she spoke more slowly. She only allowed herself the one small hope that at least she wouldn't have to go back to the cockroaches.

Fortune was at Franklin for two more weeks. During that time, her father was extradited back to Madison for forgery and theft charges, and Fortune's mother decided to move back to Iowa with the children to live with family while her husband was in jail. Fortune quickly accepted this third change of plans and told me the house would be right across the street from her school. She thought that was amazing. Much of Fortune's life seemed to be spent imagining the next place she would live.

In our last week together, Fortune would get up suddenly in the middle of a lesson and hug me tight. "Oh-hhhh. I'm going to *miss* you!"

In that last week her written sentences were never about the books we read. They were litanies that helped her deal with how difficult it would be to move:

I'm going to miss my Reading Recovery teacher.
I'm going to miss my teacher.
I'm moving next Friday.
I'm going to take my Reading Recovery teacher with me.

During her last week at school, Fortune kept asking me to give her a present. I wouldn't give her a material one, because I knew it would soon be lost and because I wanted her to real-ize that she had already received an important gift. Every time she asked me for a present I'd tell her, "I already gave you one. I taught you to read. The present's right in your head, and you'll have that with you always."

Fortune graduated from Reading Recovery the day before she left school. Her reading tested at end-of-first-grade level when she was about three-fourths of the way through first grade. She could now write fifty-two words in ten minutes (she had started with seven) and hear thirty-five out of thirty-seven sounds in a dictation. In fifty-seven lessons over seventeen weeks, she had accelerated from the bottom of her class to reading just above average for her grade. I was fairly confident her skills were strong enough that she would keep them.

On her last day of school, Fortune said good-bye over and over to her classroom teacher, to me, and to the friends she had made in school. She made excuses five times to come to my room to see me, and her classroom teacher was kind enough to let her come every time. She wrote me a card with hearts on it telling me she loved me and brought that to me. She broke away from her class and hugged me when she saw me in the hall.

That afternoon I had recess duty about an hour and a half before school was out. Fortune ran up to me, intense and excited. "HEY! DID YOU KNOW THAT WHEN IT'S WINTER IN ONE PART OF THE WORLD, IT'S *SUMMER* IN THE OTHER PART? DID YOU *KNOW* THAT?" And right away she ran off again to play.

Fortune was in anguish about leaving. But learning was such a feast for her that it overtook anything else happening in her life. Fortune's intensity and excitement made you remember what it felt like to be a kid. I loved watching her run from me, watching her decide to just enjoy being a kid playing on her last afternoon at the school.

But after recess, the rest of the day crashed down on her. In the last half hour of school, she brought a book back to me that she had borrowed. This was now our sixth farewell. More hugs, more remembrance.

Her teacher told me after school that on her way back from my room Fortune started crying in the hall. A parent found her, tears streaming down, fists clenched, pacing back and forth because she couldn't stop crying, and she couldn't bring herself to go back into her classroom crying. The parent helped Fortune back into her room, embarrassed, enduring crying. She hugged her teacher: "I've just got to hug you, I'm going to miss you so much!" Now the teacher was crying. Now children in the class were crying.

Fortune was this little con who had arrived in a fury, bustling in to steal what she could, defensive and vulnerable. By the time she left, she had our hearts. (Except Anna's. Fortune never did like Anna.) Fortune was a breath of life, predictable only in her excitment about things.

I went out to the buses to say good-bye. There she was, next to the window, tears streaming down. She looked at me, overcome. I got on the bus, pushing past children fooling in the aisle until I got to the back where Fortune sat. I hugged her one more time. She looked at me, unable to speak by now, and just held on tight to me. She was disintegrating.

The bus driver was waiting to leave. I got off the bus and stood outside her window as she looked at me, crying. By now I was crying, too, as I stood there watching her pull away.

Nicholas
A Writer's Son

A lot of teachers knew Nicholas because they knew his older sister, Karin. When people talked about her, they always called her "a real brain." She amazed teachers in the way she learned beyond her years. She had her own way, and she seemed to come at things from a tangent. Karin didn't learn the way you expected her to when you taught.

Nicholas's father was a well-known regional writer; although he was friendly, his mind sometimes seemed elsewhere when he talked with you. Nicholas was in awe of his father, and I think even at times afraid of him because Nicholas was so worried about letting his dad down.

His mother was back in graduate school now that Nicholas was in school. Nicholas was particularly proud that she had a beeper that she carried around with her at the university. He knew he could always reach her that way. Though Nicholas's father seemed present but absent when he talked to you, Nicholas's mother was there in every way she could be. She loved Nicholas deeply and knew he wasn't doing well. She was a calm, gracious woman, ready to work on any suggestion we had that might help Nicholas.

Nicholas was from a highly literate family with high expectations. He was at the bottom of his class.

It's apt to describe Nicholas first in terms of others, because that is how Nicholas saw himself. He was failing in school, and he was painfully aware of his own failure and others' success.

Nicholas knew he wasn't learning how to read. To measure how badly he was doing, he carefully observed what other children were reading and memorized what their books looked like. Then, for free reading time in class, Nicholas chose the same books for himself, books he saw the other children reading successfully.

But he could never read these books. He sat in class holding books he knew he couldn't decipher. As the months went by, the books he held became increasingly beyond his reach. Each day Nicholas sat watching others and gauging his failure. He kept choosing harder books, rubbing salt in his wound. He put tremendous pressure on himself and accepted his failure only by knowing its detail and judging it severely.

He was withdrawn, nervous, unsure of himself, and sad. We saw it on his face; his parents saw it on his face. He had thick blond hair that emphasized his forehead and drew you to his clear blue eyes. Nicholas's eyes were ruefully vulnerable. They showed how difficult it was for him to be in school and not do well. Nicholas used a lot of courage every day.

At times, almost out of character with his sadness but not his unease, he would suddenly act goofy to cover up his embarrassment and the insufficiency he saw in himself. He would draw attention to himself like this as a catharsis and then withdraw again. He wasn't getting work done in class. And every day when he went home, he measured himself against every other successful family member. Especially Karin; he failed in her shadow.

I began working with Nicholas in the last quarter of the year. He wasn't a child who would have come up for Reading Recovery at the beginning of the year because he was articulate and bright and had grown up around books. But by the time I started working with him, he had fallen behind all but two kids in his class, one of whom I was already teaching in Reading Recovery. If Nicholas didn't learn with me, he would probably end up in the learning disabilities program. And with his fragile sense of self, I was afraid he would just sink lower there.

When we started working together, Nicholas had good skills, but he couldn't apply them. He knew all his ABCs. He could write several words but couldn't read them back. He corrected errors well on easy books (a self-correction for every error), but when the books became a little more difficult, his self-corrections all but stopped. He made only one correction for every twenty-seven errors. Books became like a Lewis Carroll poem for him, but he trudged on even so, speaking nonsense.

Though it was a good sign that Nicholas could self-correct well on easy books, this indicated another problem. Nicholas corrected errors well because he made a lot of them, and used to defeating himself, he was closely aware of what he did wrong. When I first began working with him, this intense awareness of his errors was what would eventually wear him down. His reading then would quickly change from coherent to awful.

There was another anomaly in Nicholas's learning. Though his teacher had worked with Nicholas all year on his writing, close to the end of first grade he still wrote almost exclusively in capital letters. For a child as aware of himself as Nicholas was, it was surprising that he couldn't do something as seemingly simple as writing with lowercase letters that he knew how to form. This was a flag about Nicholas and his survival in school. It was as if he knew writing in lowercase was going to be difficult for him so he had sequestered it. He made a conscious choice not to write in lowercase letters so that he didn't fail in that, too. He kept himself from drowning by not attempting to swim.

I thought about his sister as I taught him, about how everyone said how bright and tangential she was. Karin had somehow figured out how to see things askance and bring them around, so she learned what was required and more. Nicholas couldn't do this. Each day as I watched him learning, I realized that Nicholas needed to be taught to see his own way, to learn how he learned.

In our first weeks together Nicholas was willing to come with me, but he was wary of me, too. He knew that working with me meant he wasn't doing well. As we worked in Roaming Around the Known, I could tell he was annoyed by the books we read; they looked like baby books to him. One day he balked at them and told me he wanted to read harder books. I put aside the book I had asked him to read and turned to him.

This was the most important talk Nicholas and I had in our month and a half together because it gave him a chance to feel different about himself in school. I told him I thought he was smart. Nicholas jumped a bit—it was a visible shock to him. I told him again I thought he was smart and that it must be very hard on him not to be able to read easily. Nicholas looked at me oddly, wanting to believe me and trying to figure out the con. But he let me see what he looked like when he wasn't failing.

I walked across the room to my bookshelf and got out some second-grade trade books. "You want to read books like these, don't you?" Nicholas nodded at me. I went back and sat so that I looked right in his face and he right in mine. I told him that I wanted him to read them, too, but that he just had to trust me. I was giving him easy books because I wanted him to be able to read the hard ones. That's where we were aiming, and I could teach him best this way.

Nicholas was amazed. It was as if he had thought he was invisible and then realized someone had just seen him. Nicholas's teacher cares tremendously about her students, takes them home in her head, and worries about them as she falls asleep at night. Throughout the year she had repeatedly tried to get him to see himself differently, easier. But for Nicholas the isolation of Reading Recovery, away from other children's opinions or eavesdropping, was critical. In the separateness of my room Nicholas could accept what I said. No one overheard that I thought he was smart, so he didn't have to prove it right away. I told him he would have to trust me. He looked at me, solemn and hopeful; he decided he would.

Nicholas threw himself into reading and proving himself to me, and he even risked proving himself to himself. Once I set him free by giving him hope, he worked as hard as he could to learn as much as he could. I read trade books like *Five Little Monkeys Jumping on the Bed* by Eileen Christelow and *Goodnight Moon* by Margaret W. Brown to him, and he listened and watched intently, determined to take over the reading. The words in *Goodnight Moon* change slightly from page to page. He searched the pictures carefully, then checked the words to make sure he said the right thing. He loved the empty page "Goodnight nobody," enjoying its humor. *Goodnight Moon* was far beyond what Nicholas could read independently, but reading it over and over with me and essentially memorizing it gave him a confidence I had never before seen on his face. Everything Nicholas did and felt was written on his face in those days.

For the first time, he began to persevere after making errors, something difficult for a boy as hard on himself as Nicholas. "Off-to-flat-fast" he read for *fast*, making four attempts until he knew it was right. In the security of our room, he was giving everything he had to learning to read. Together we wrote "Where's Nicholas?" just as Fortune had written "Where's Fortune?" When most children write this book, a monster (or a parent) is looking for them. For Nicholas, it was an entire army: "An army is looking for Nicholas." It seemed to me to represent how school felt to Nicholas, an entire army searching for him, looking for his failure.

Nicholas's book was different in another way. His sentences showed a wider experience and a much more extended vocabulary and knowledge than most of my Reading Recovery students' books. Most children make up sentences that describe known places around home or school. In their books, they hide in a closet, under a bed, or behind a door. In Nicholas's book, he wrote sentences such as "Is he in the Statue of Liberty?" "Is he in the White House?" As he continued to write the book, Nicholas took himself to the Empire State Building, the Great Wall of China, and finally Korea before the final question that returned him home: "Is he in his house?" As the book got longer, Nicholas seemed to change from the victim the army was hunting down to the hero who outwitted it. He enjoyed running his army of observers all over the world and then bringing them back home to find him in the most obvious place. In the process of writing this book, Nicholas opened up with me.

In the sixth Roaming session we looked at *I've Been Eating Blackberries* by Alan Trussell-Cullen. As I talked about the pictures, he put his finger under each word on the page, intent on internalizing the meaning and the words. When I finished talking about the book, Nicholas looked up at me and said, "OK, now I can try it." This confidence that he could actually attempt something was new for him.

Now by the end of each session, Nicholas was putting the books he could read in a careful pile, counting them off. We were up to ten books, and he was relieved to feel such accomplishment. He would look up at me sheepishly, uncomfortable with feeling so happy about himself. He would sigh with pride as he put the last book on the table, nodding his head, looking surprised.

But this was no miraculous transformation. A week alone with a reading teacher had not made him a different child. Nicholas still had days where he fell far back. In his eighth Roaming session, Nicholas read for the first time a humorous book in which bigger and bigger animals get angry at each other. He was reading it very well, when suddenly everything about him changed. In a matter of seconds, he lost confidence and was clearly in acute pain. He manifested a headache. I have never seen a child look so ill so quickly. It told volumes about the pressure inside Nicholas as he urged himself on to learn.

We stopped reading, and I told him he looked like he didn't feel well. He told me about his headache and how often he gets them in school. He was very frank and matter-of-fact; this was just reality for him. This kind of headache came when he didn't know a word and started worrying about it. I told him how well he was doing and that we would work on taking pressure off him. We didn't read any more that day. Nicholas was clearly in too much pain. But I slowly repeated how well I thought he was doing. It became almost a chant, a sound to ease the pain. Nicholas went back to class knowing I accepted him.

After he left I went over the lesson in my head, trying to figure out why Nicholas had suddenly felt so ill. I realized that although I had been trying to pump Nicholas up by telling him how well he did, he only felt that praise as more pressure. For a child like Nicholas, praise can be as deadly as criticism. Because he didn't believe in himself yet, he thought he had somehow fooled me—that I thought he was doing well when he really wasn't. I had put Nicholas in a double bind: either he had to work much harder to become as good as I seemed to mistakenly think he already was, or he'd reveal himself and I'd realize he wasn't doing well after all. I would see through him and realize he was still a failure. No wonder he had a headache.

For the rest of our time together, I had to find the balance between letting Nicholas work as hard as he wanted to and making him feel he had to work even harder. With a child like Nicholas, it is difficult to instill confidence without overly heightening his expectations of himself.

I pulled back and stopped overtly praising him. Instead, I asked him each day how he thought he had done. Without the pressure of what he saw as undeserved praise, Nicholas could see himself more clearly. He now began to say that he thought he was doing OK. This became a ritual every day. The less I said the better.

In the aggregate Nicholas knew much more about reading than the other students I taught. He could hear sounds well, he read for meaning, and he monitored words as he read. But what he knew stayed in isolated pieces, as my other students read harder books. As long as he continued to be unsure of himself, Nicholas couldn't seem to use the knowledge he had to put the pieces together so he could read. But he was also unsure of himself because he couldn't read.

Many of the qualities that Nicholas brought to failure and confusion—introspection, independence, awareness of detail—eventually helped him learn to read and to believe in himself. I just had to find the key. Nicholas was caught in a paradox: to succeed in school, he needed to succeed by his own demanding standards. He had to find a way to let himself learn. Which meant I had to find a way to let him learn.

By the end of our Roaming sessions Nicholas had gained noticeable confidence. He loved the pile of books he could make and read one by one. He would look up at me smiling large when he had the pile perfectly stacked. He could now write and read thirty-two words, up six from two weeks before. He read with expression, enjoying books. But he was still writing in uppercase letters unless prompted to write in lowercase. And though he understood the process of writing words generated from a similar ending like *cat, sat,* and *mat,* he couldn't read them back once written. It was again the problem he had of knowing parts but not the whole.

And so we began formal lessons. Nicholas read the first book I gave him, *Moonlight* by Marcia Vaughn, easily and with expression. Two weeks earlier this book would have crushed him. But now he brought more confidence to what he read.

One of the pleasures of teaching Nicholas was that he had a large vocabulary. I could give him books with poetic imagery, and he would respond to the sound of the language. Sentences such as "The moon is lighting the bay" and "The moon is shining on the creek" led him to linger over pictures and enjoy the subtle differences from page to page. With my other students, trying to read words like *bay* and *creek* that weren't in their vocabulary just made them feel insecure and slowed them down in reading. But with his large vocabulary, Nicholas could enjoy books that were a stretch for him and that looked literary. My choice of the more poetic books in my collection for Nicholas helped him feel more confident. They looked more like the books he was watching other kids read in class, and he felt he was making progress.

We moved quickly through book levels, spending one, two, or at the most three days on each. When Nicholas began reading with me, he read well for meaning and looked enough at words to know if he was reading them wrong. If a word was wrong, Nicholas would try again to get it right. But he wasn't seeing the whole word or the letters in sequence well enough to read it correctly. For *tiptoe* he first read "stepping," then seeing the error he tried "torptoe-talp-talping." He finally gave up, realizing that what he was saying didn't make sense. He used syntax well, though, and he often made errors that sounded right and used the right first letter, like "along" for *across*.

Nicholas's mother came to see our fourth lesson. Nicholas now felt like he could do things, and he was excited his mother was there. She and I doted on him, both feeling a mother's pride in a child who is finally succeeding. I had been working for the past three days on getting Nicholas to understand the concept of generating words so that he could learn to read the words he could generate in writing. At the beginning of the lesson I asked him to write *day* and then *way* on the board. He did it successfully and then turned to his mother, chalk still in his hand, intoning like a teacher, "See, if I can write *day,* I can write *way* because they both end the same." He had internalized what he had been taught and knew it was a strategy to use. Nicholas beamed. His mother beamed. I beamed.

After that day with his mother, when Nicholas realized he understood how to apply the concept of generating words, he watched and listened to me differently. It was a change similar to the one that occurred after our first real talk when I had asked Nicholas to trust me. There was something very adult about Nicholas now; he was serious, patient, and intent. He would look at me silently, taking in everything I said. He stared at me, and yet he was very internal as he did it. He began to approach reading as if it were something he thought he was capable of.

As he became more sure, I backed further away, respecting the independence he was showing. I said less in our lessons, and I gave him even more time to figure things out. I would move my chair back and sit back in my chair as he began to read, giving him physical space, too. His reading became a ritual, his incantation in learning. I felt like a catalyst. I fed him the minimum that he needed and watched him take off.

A crucial reason why Nicholas made such rapid progress in Reading Recovery was that he was able to turn something that was making him fail—intense observation of his errors— into a strategy for successful reading. As we move children through the lessons of Reading Recovery, a main focus is to teach them to check one system of language (meaning, structure, and visual representation) against another as they read. Nicholas had always done this cross-checking, but it had made him give up because he saw he was doing something wrong. Now, alone with a teacher giving him just enough but not too much of a challenge, he was able to turn his constant checking on himself into a way of seeing what he did right.

When we first started working together, Nicholas read mostly for meaning and didn't look at words closely enough to read them correctly. As he became more aware of the importance of looking at the whole word, his errors and his reading switched briefly to being based mainly on reading the word in isolation; he forgot the importance of meaning as he read. He read "be-tord-torger-toeger-togther-toe-toegeether-torger" for *together.* Children commonly make these shifts in emphasis as they learn to read.

Nicholas learned the right balance between reading for meaning and reading for what the word looks like by learning to scan across words to see part and letter order. He started seeing chunks in words: *all* in *allowed, can* in *candy.* He learned to say a hard word slowly, working on getting every sound right and in order and correcting what didn't look or sound right: "k-ch-chilps-chips" for *chips,* "bud-dud-dad" for *dad.* Once Nicholas learned these skills of looking for chunks and saying a word slowly, he went back to reading for meaning and continued his rapid progress.

By the twelfth lesson I was confident that Nicholas would graduate from Reading Recovery. I was by now very attached to Nicholas and loved watching how he was finding his own way out of insecurity. Nicholas was large for his age, looked older than he was, and in his unsureness kept a distance. Nothing about him invited a hug or an arm around his shoulder. But he wanted the attention, he just didn't know how to ask for it. At the end of every lesson I would ask Nicholas how he thought he had done. Because he was doing well, he would now each day tell me that. I would nod my head and say I thought so, too, and then pull him in to a hug. Soon Nicholas was initiating the hug by shuffling to my chair each day, eyes down, looking embarrassed—then melting into the hug and not wanting to let go of me. When he did let go he'd look at me, embarrassed again but smiling, and then walk out the door, shaking his head.

Nicholas, with so much going for him in terms of family, affluence, and intelligence, had almost condemned himself to failure in school. I knew now he would read, but I wanted to make sure that he was aware that he could apply what he had done in learning to read to learning in general.

As we went through the lessons so quickly, I was struck over and over by Nicholas's independence and ability to integrate learning once he trusted himself. Just as he had assimilated how to generate words, a few weeks later he absorbed the rule of silent *e,* something that most kids learn over weeks or months. I can still see him silently nodding his head yes as I explained it to him. I taught it at the end of a lesson; two days later it was a part of his fluent reading.

I mentioned to Nicholas that most children couldn't use a rule like that so quickly. At the end of that lesson, I also told him he was independent and that quality made him a strong learner. "Do you know what *independent* means?" I asked. ("No.") I told him that it meant he did things on his own, that he relied on himself a lot, that this was something to know about himself and be proud of.

I told Nicholas we were going up to the library together before he went back to class. We walked to Webster's unabridged dictionary, a tome on a corner bookstand with the aura of Merlin's library. To a seven-year-old, this book must look unapproachable, crammed with little words in columns, no clear space between them. I hoped this made it seem momentous.

I told Nicholas how much I loved dictionaries and loved to find words in them. I told him it was important for us to look up the word *independent,* because it was a word I wanted him to be sure to know. I didn't find the exact definition I wanted, but I took what was close enough and copied it on a piece of paper for Nicholas: "Not depending on others for the formation of opinions or guidance of conduct. Thinking or acting, or disposed to think or act, for oneself."

"Here, Nicholas, this is for you to keep and know about yourself. You're independent, Nicholas, and you do much of your learning on your own. Don't forget that. It's a great way to learn. Show this to your parents tonight, and have them read it to you again."

Nicholas was embarrassed but loved the attention, so I didn't let up on him. We took his paper back to his teacher, and Nicholas showed it to her and told her what *independent* means (eyes down, mumbling but happy). She told him that's what she saw in him, too. Nicholas was radiant. We admired him some more—the genuine praise didn't overwhelm him now—and we felt giddy at the change we had helped bring about in him.

There was only one day in our twenty-one lessons when Nicholas read below 90 percent accuracy for his daily Running Record. We had had an assembly that morning, and Nicholas's Reading Recovery time spilled over into recess. We kept working, but Nicholas's mind was on recess so he didn't read carefully and made foolish errors.

But his rushing was also a sign of how much learning to read was changing Nicholas. Before, recess hadn't mattered much to him because he was unsure of himself and so remained a loner. He would walk slowly to recess to lean against the playground fence by himself until the bell rang. Then he would walk slowly back into the school. Now he wanted to get out there and play soccer as hard as he could— Nicholas was finding his place. I made him finish his work and then followed him to the playground.

It was a cool, sunny spring day, with a breeze in the air that made you feel warmer after winter. Nicholas didn't notice I was there. He was laughing and running, guiding the soccer ball down the playground. Nicholas was happy.

In his final lessons Nicholas read a harder book each time, still making some errors, but also making visible progress in applying what he had learned. If he reached a point where what he said didn't make sense, he would back up in the sentence and start again, a clear sign that he was using meaning and structure in approaching words. He was confident; he was independent; he was relieved.

In our six weeks together, I taught Nicholas and Nicholas taught me. I'm good at praising children, telling them what I see in them and that I value it. With Nicholas I learned how too much praise can be a burden to children. To let him learn, I had to learn to back away, to stop talking.

Acceptance differs from child to child. Fortune needed praise repeated and repeated. It made her feel seen. But Nicholas needed distance and silence. Praise made him feel counterfeit because he didn't believe it.

Once I understood this response, I felt a tangible calm in teaching Nicholas. We found our rhythm, and I established a place for him to feel confident and unpressured as he progressed with incredible speed. As the days went by, I became very aware that I felt this calm because I was in the presence of learning. I was guiding but not controlling it. There was a clarity, and it was all because Nicholas was finding what it was like to believe in himself.

By the time Nicholas left Reading Recovery, he had changed in school. He had friends in class. He got his work done. He smiled with ease. He thought he was capable. This was the most important change—he thought he was capable. After twenty-one lessons (the norm is sixty), he graduated from Reading Recovery able to read books from the end of first grade very well. He was a changed boy.

Nicholas continued to do well in second grade and confidently read books written for much older kids. When I checked Nicholas's reading at the end of second grade, he could read sixth-grade texts.

In a school like Franklin the children from real poverty are given a chance. They go to a middle-class school with resources unheard-of in poor neighborhoods. They are loved and expected to do well, and because of these two factors, they generally do. But it is not only poor children who can lead difficult lives. Nicholas, the sad, insecure son of an accomplished writer, attests to that.

Most children at the bottom of their class have more obvious things against them than Nicholas did. To teach him,

I had to give him both himself and books. But for all children, in less extreme ways, love of learning is tied to their sense of themselves. If they don't feel worthy or capable of succeeding, they won't succeed.

Kareem
From the Chicago Projects

Kareem T. Little. One of the kids I've loved the most in teaching. A beautiful, large smile, eyes dancing as he led you on with it. Brown skin so perfect it almost shone. I never think of Kareem sitting still because he hardly ever did. I see him gliding past, on his way somewhere—probably trouble—deciding whether in that instant to connect or not. He usually did with me. His eyes would see right into mine, because he loved me, too. And then he'd move on.

Kareem had come to Franklin School the year before in kindergarten from a homeless program. He didn't know what ghetto in Chicago he had lived in, but he knew he was lucky to be away from it. When his family first arrived in Madison, they stayed in a homeless shelter, and then the entire family of eight had moved into a motel room on the outskirts of town. The kids had to run across an expressway to catch a bus to school each day. Kareem hadn't spent his early childhood being read to, going to preschool, or watching the latest Disney movie. He knew struggle.

Kareem was one of those students whose reputation precedes him. I had been told he was "challenging," a teacher euphemism for real behavior problems. By Wednesday of the first week of school, the children in Kareem's class were already tired of him. He bonked them on the head, kicked them under the table, stole their pencils when they weren't— or were—looking. Kareem was so good at being the bad boy that even if he was out of the room when a problem happened kids would indignantly and righteously shout, "Kareem did it!" He soon had no friends.

I met Kareem in that first week. His teacher and I knew I'd be working with him in Reading Recovery, so the first Thursday of school when the whole school took a field trip (walking two blocks to see the circus leave town) I went with Kareem's class to get to know Kareem and to ride herd on him, too.

Shortly before we left, his teacher introduced me to Kareem. As we walked out of the building, Kareem both showed me he was aware of me and ignored me, alternating between the two. He would try to connect with me, charm me, and then be off on something else. Because he had a teacher for a partner, he restrained his speed, but you could tell that without me he would have been long ahead of his class, racing to be the first to see whatever was there.

We talked as we walked. About the day, about circuses, about his family, about Kareem. He was warming up to me, starting to become interested in me because I was clearly interested in him. After a while, I stopped having to ask him questions, because he was amazed to have a teacher paying attention to him when he wasn't in trouble. He would talk readily until he was distracted by something else.

Franklin is in the middle of an older, working-class neighborhood. It's a good, quiet neighborhood; many retired people have stayed there in their homes after their families have grown and moved on. We were walking down the first block away from Franklin when several houses ahead of us a frail-looking man, probably in his eighties, opened his front door and started slowly navigating out of it with a walker. It was meticulous, difficult work for him, and Kareem noticed him right away.

He pointed to the man and looked at me, confident. "I know what that is," he said. "My cousin got one of those." I wasn't sure what he meant at first but then realized he was talking about the walker.

It was a glorious, sunny day, a perfect day to see a circus train. The road the circus was leaving town on has a large grassy area along its edge, and Franklin's five hundred students soon filled it up. The students were divided into groups of classes, with teachers and parents constantly counting and recounting heads to make sure everyone was there. We were on time, but the circus wasn't.

Kareem sat obediently, pleasingly, for about three minutes, but then it was just too long for him not to be moving. "Look at this," he said, and he shot away from me, back to an open grassy space where there were no kids.

He started with cartwheels, one after another, legs and arms sweeping easy and straight into a rotating X. He smiled as he turned over and over with ease. This was Kareem at his best, and he loved the freedom of shining. Turning, turning, he watched me watch him. He walked around on both hands, he walked on one hand, the grass giving enough bounce for him to keep going. "Watch this." Smiling, he took a running start and then did a flip, circling over in the air, arms crossed confidently across his chest. Checking to see if I was still watching, he ran and vaulted again. He loved not touching the ground.

He walked back toward me, looking around, realizing other kids were watching him. In four days of school, this was the first time any of them had seen Kareem both do something well and be out of trouble. He was embarrassed and pleased, eyes down, strutting.

The circus came, and we watched it, sun glinting in our eyes. The children were amazed at wild animals so close. Lions and tigers pacing in cages, staring out as they rolled along. Huge elephants slowly plodding past, oblivious to us, trunks moving rhythmically in the heat. Ostriches on leashes bobbing past—all almost close enough to touch. Kareem stood next to me as the circus left. He stayed still long enough to watch the animals and to decide maybe to trust me. When the circus had passed, he and I walked back to school as partners again. Kareem, finally relaxed, restrained himself from zooming ahead. We were friends, at least for right now.

When we begin work with Reading Recovery students, we send home permission slips for the students to be in the program. Usually we phone first, introducing ourselves to the parents, explaining the program, and answering any questions.

Kareem's family had no phone, so the Monday after the circus train I sent a note home with the permission slip, describing the program and asking if I could come talk with his parents on Wednesday. Permission came right back, but when I asked Kareem if I could come to his house the next day, he said quickly, "No! They said they gotta scrub!" I could come on Friday, but not until then. This seemed a good beginning to me. They clearly cared I was coming.

Kareem's house was a large, run-down, comfortable house on a dead end, mixed in with light industry in an old part of the city. Panes of glass were missing in the house's storm door. The doorbell no longer worked. But this house must have looked and felt like paradise after a high-rise ghetto apartment in Chicago and homelessness in Madison.

They *had* scrubbed. Not a dish on the counter in the kitchen. Chairs pushed in to tables, no clutter, nothing out of place. I was led, pleasantries and nodding all around, through the dining room and past Kareem's cousin, who was sitting doing the ironing. He was starching shirts, and he was the one with the walker. He seemed to be in his early twenties, and he was a large, strong-looking man. He looked totally out of place, sitting with his iron and his ironing board. I had since learned that he had been shot in the back in their Chicago apartment and that Kareem had witnessed the shooting. We were introduced, and then I was taken to another room so Kareem's mother and I could talk.

I was a teacher at their home, and Kareem wasn't in trouble. Everyone was pleased by this, so we gushed on both sides. I told his mother that I thought Kareem was smart and that he could learn to read with this program. She was surprised and even a little taken aback by my statement. She told me she had never thought he was as smart as her other kids.

I showed her the kind of books we would be using and explained the work they would need to do at home with him each night. She smiled, I smiled, Kareem smiled. This was a great day, and this kid was going to succeed. We talked as mothers. Kareem's mother told me about her other children, and I told her about mine. Then we reached the point where there was nothing more to be said. I walked back out past the cousin, still ironing next to his walker. We nodded and smiled.

Kareem had painfully low skills in most areas when we started out. He couldn't read the easiest pattern we ask kids to read—"No. No. No." on a page in *Where's Spot?* He could identify only about 60 percent of the letters in the alphabet. When I asked him to write as many words as he could, he initially wrote, "L P O E T." It was my first time giving this test, and I was excited that a first-grader could write *poet* until it became clear Kareem was writing random letters. The words he could write and read back were *Kareem, dog, to,* and *stop.* He also wrote his last name, Little, but read it back as his middle name, Tarif.

What stood out for a kid at the bottom of his class at the beginning of first grade was that he understood significant concepts about books. He could locate the front of a book, and he understood that print contains a message. He knew where to start reading on a page, which direction to read in, and what were the first and last parts of a page. When I pointed to capital letters on a page, he could show me the corresponding lowercase letters: *t* for *T*, *b* for *B*. He could isolate one and two letters on a page, but not one and two words. When he wrote, he formed his letters clearly and spaced them well. He left space between words, showing that he did understand some difference between words and letters.

But compounding Kareem's low reading skills were his other problems. He was poor, so poor that he had been homeless, and now that he had a home he was still often hungry. And he was always in trouble. His acting up kept him from learning and, just as important, kept him from becoming attached to people. School was no treat for him. He got through his days there by keeping his distance and failing by choice.

However, dangling in front of him was the lure of this one teacher who appeared every day and wanted to spend time with just him. I was amazing to Kareem. I broke up his long day with a half hour when he was in the spotlight.

So when we started Roaming Around the Known, Kareem was intent on pleasing me. He wanted to show me everything he knew, which is exactly the purpose of Roaming. On our first day, I read a short book, called *Look...* (The Wright Group) to him. As soon as he saw the pattern that repeated on each page, he took over and then read the book a second time alone. Together we wrote the sentence "Kareem likes dogs" on the board. Then Kareem dashed back to our table, picked up *Look...*, and read it to me again. I read him another short book, *I Like...* (The Wright Group), and as I did, he sat close to me, reaching out and holding the book with me. He turned the pages as I read and then tried to predict the sentences before I said them. At the end of our session, when I asked him to read *I Like...* once more, he very seriously, like a magician before a difficult trick, picked up both *Look...* and *I Like...*, put them in a meticulous pile and then read both to me.

Kareem had just spent a half hour trying to do well, not his usual behavior in school. I took him back to his room, his hand locked in mine so that he would stay with me in the hall and could bask in my praise. I told him to show his teacher his books and read them to her, and shy, beaming, and embarrassed, he did. We both praised him, and I left the room. Without the constant individual attention, however, he was soon back in trouble. But he had had several minutes that day when he was out of trouble. His classroom teacher and I had given him a big enough chance to be someone different in school, and he had briefly taken it.

When Kareem came to my room the next day, he smiled as soon as he saw *Look...*, and read it on his own, twice. Kareem was increasingly drawn to books during our two weeks of Roaming. Each time I introduced a new book, he wanted to read it over and over. In addition, when he made errors he began noticing them and even began self-correcting, an essential skill that the leisurely pace of the early weeks of Reading Recovery was allowing him to learn.

In our third session we went back to the book *Where's Spot?* We had read this together when I first observed him. This time as I pointed, he started to notice how many times the word *no* was on a page. In our fourth session he was so involved with the book that each time he read the word *no* he tried to sound like the animal who was speaking. Kareem was in turn a snake, a hippopotamus, a lion, and monkeys. Because he was interested, he was unconsciously starting to give himself a chance in school.

On his first day with me when we had written together "Kareem likes dogs," I had shown him that by adding *s* to *dog* (which he knew how to write) he could write another word, *dogs.* In this session, three days later, when he read *dogs* in *Look,* he stopped, checked the word closely for the final *s* and said, "Yep, *dogs.*" Together we wrote the sentence "Kareem Little likes dogs and cats and," and I asked him to name something else he liked. He rushed to the board for magnetic letters, finishing the sentence with "aabb AABBDD."

Kareem was excited and engaged, but it was clear that he still was confused by the difference between words and letters. He hadn't yet understood that written words represent the sounds of the names we give to things.

Our new book in the fourth session was *My Family* (The Wright Group), a little book with African American characters. As soon as we finished it, he beamed and said, "I gotta read this again!" turning as fast as he could to the front of the book. This book offered another link to school for Kareem, with its characters that were closer to his own experience.

But after the first week of Roaming sessions, Kareem had had enough of company behavior. He started acting really squirrelly, jumping up and pacing around, talking a mile a minute. I had a yardstick and pointer as part of the materials in the room. The other kids I taught hadn't even noticed them. Kareem would grab them and sprint to the board, pointing and pretending he was a teacher. Since we got along so well, Kareem had decided that time with me was definitely for play and he would be in charge. During the entire year we spent together, there was a fine line between showing Kareem the acceptance he needed to succeed in school and keeping him in line so that he could focus enough to learn. I hid the yardstick and pointer on a shelf eight feet high. I took anything that would distract him out of the room. And I started teaching with my arm warmly but firmly around his shoulder to keep him in his seat.

In our seventh Roaming session we ran into a problem that would plague Kareem throughout the year: his limited vocabulary. We were reading a book about zoo animals, and Kareem, a seven-year-old in first grade, didn't know the words *rhinoceros* and *giraffe*. Clearly they were not a part of his daily life, but most children are interested enough in these strange animals to know the words for them before kindergarten. Outside of school Kareem had had little exposure to anything beyond daily life. His smaller vocabulary, his inability to simply name as many things as other kids, in itself put him behind.

In our eighth session, when reading *My Family* once again, Kareem noticed that the word for the father was *Father,* not *Dad,* which had been his first reading. This was solid evidence that Kareem was looking at and thinking about the words on the page. All through Roaming I saw these incremental steps that meant real progress.

Kareem could be quite funny. In our ninth session, when reading *I Like...* for what seemed to him like the four-hundredth time, he skipped a page, noticed it, and went back and corrected. Then, in exactly the same intonation he had used for the patterned reading, he pretended to read, "I like to skip pages."

But he could quickly cross from humor to acting out. It was a problem we had the entire year. No one put him to bed at home, and like any first-grader, he couldn't concentrate when he was tired. A few minutes after carefully reading his imaginary page, Kareem became unfocused and uncooperative, distancing and distracting himself from what he was doing. He stopped looking at the book and made up text, except there was no humor to it now. He covered the words with his hand and looked at the ceiling as he pretended to read. I spent most of the session pulling him back to task. When I asked him what time he went to bed, he said, "You know. It starts with a *t.*" Then, though we were reading, he grabbed a dry-erase board and started writing. Once he became so random, it was uphill work trying to bring him back.

At the end of Roaming, Kareem still confused letters and words. But he had started to look at words, and he could read several small books. His writing vocabulary had grown by two words: he could now write *Kareem, dog, stop, no, go,* and *I.* (On that day he could no longer write *to.*) He also was used to being with me away from class.

However, when formal instruction began and each day Kareem had to read for the Running Record with no support from me, it was obvious that he still was not really looking at the words on the page. In the first lesson he read "Here go my dog" for the phrase "My puppy." He didn't notice that he read four words when there were only two. If children don't learn to look at words, they don't learn to read.

When I first started teaching reading, I thought that letter-sound knowledge—to an adult the most obvious aspect of reading—was the most important part of instruction. You taught children letters, the sounds of the letters, and then the sounds in words. Children *do* need to learn letters and their sounds, and most children learn them in kindergarten or before. But the task of reading is not primarily decoding; it is making *meaning* out of what is written. Phonics and phonology are primarily systems of sound correlation.

When children and adults read well, they are reading at a high level of meaning, and what they read makes sense. Drawing unconsciously on and repeatedly integrating meaning, structure, and the written word, fluent adult readers scan groups of words as they read. If meaning breaks down, they will read more slowly, go back and reread a sentence, segment words into syllables in order to read them more carefully, look up a word in a dictionary, or use some combination of these strategies. They do not sound out a word letter by letter, because that is not meaningful.

Most children in learning to read do need to pass through some stage of learning to sound out or visually analyze words. It is an important part of seeing the whole. But this process is most powerfully taught in the context of higher-level strategic questions ("Does that make sense?" "What word would I expect that to be?") so that children are from the beginning learning to think about meaning while keeping track of words.

We teach this awareness in Reading Recovery by making sure the children are conscious that they are reading the page in front of them. Pointing to words encourages them to focus on seeing words in order on a page. The repetition and the rhythm of the pointing physically involve the child in seeing reading as a progression. Because we are always asking questions about the picture, too ("Does that make sense?" "Do you see that in the picture?"), they see the words as holding meaning.

This is the metaphysics of reading, the quest from beginning to end. But the physical act of pointing has another important aspect. As they point, the children are drawn into the book and become attached to it. Many children who struggle in school have little experience focusing on a task and staying with it. Pointing teaches them to do the same thing again and again: to point to this word, to point to the next, to point to the next, to turn the page and point to the next. The repetition and the physical attachment to the page help them learn about what the page means. Pointing also helps them stay with reading rather than being distracted by something else.

I think that the need to focus on one thing is why it was so difficult for Kareem to learn to point correctly to words on a page. He was a distractible, kinetic child whose attention was easily drawn away from the task at hand. If Kareem was *here,* he wanted to be *there.* And suddenly was. The slow routine of pointing was anathema to his personality. But it was crucial to his learning to really look at books.

Kareem and I spent thirty-three lessons focusing on pointing to words, until I was finally sure he had learned to attend to print. He would seem to have the process under control and then would have another day when he lapsed into randomness again. So we practiced again and again. ("Read it with your finger." "Did that match?" "Go back and make it match." "Find *is.*" "Find *to.*" "Find *like.*") Until finally I knew he was looking at what he saw. At a higher level, Kareem's ability to look at print became the strongest skill he took from Reading Recovery. He had learned to closely monitor what he read, no matter how difficult, no matter how foreign the subject and the words were to him.

In the initial lessons Kareem and I also spent time adding to the number of letters in the alphabet he could recognize and use. He wrote and said, over and over, *n, l, y, k, f,* as each day we increased his knowledge of the alphabet.

Reading Recovery teaches letter knowledge in the context of reading. (This approach is the opposite of many traditional programs where reading is taught in the context of letter knowledge.) Children like Kareem who know very few letters are specifically taught letters and sounds—what letters are called, how they are formed, and words that start with them—for one or two minutes of the thirty-minute lesson. But letter knowledge is more crucially gained by seeing words in print and by thinking about words and their sounds as having meaning. So letters and sounds are fundamentally taught in Reading Recovery by asking children when they are reading what letter they would expect a word to begin with. If they don't know, we say, for example, "I hear a *b*." In this way, their learning about letters and sounds is strengthened by its attachment to meaning.

Similarly, children gain concrete letter and sound knowledge by listening for sounds in their writing. They learn to distinguish sounds in words found in sentences that they have made up, sentences that matter to them. Sound and sign are rooted in the child's own particular meaning. They are not isolated elements the child must master before being allowed to turn the pages of a book.

As we went through those thirty-three lessons making sure that Kareem really looked at what he read and that he knew more and more about letters in words, he showed that he was picking up other skills. In the seventh lesson, Kareem used a rerunning start twice, going back once to self-correct by checking the first letter after reading *elephant* instead of *lion*. This was the first time Kareem self-corrected on a Running Record. It showed he had an independence and discipline he hadn't had before.

For a kid like Kareem, the fact that he cared enough about what he was doing to try to do it right was in itself huge progress.

It was now October. His classroom teacher's clear structure for him in class and his hard work with me were paying off. He was settling down some, and kids weren't always sure it was Kareem who did something wrong. In terms of discipline, I had what was doable—half an hour a day one-on-one. His teacher had Kareem the entire rest of the day in a class full of other kids. She wasn't easy on Kareem, because he didn't need anyone to be easy on him. At the same time, she constantly showed him a lot of love. She gave him a tight structure and clear consequences for misbehaving, and he responded by acting better in class. But there were many days when the office must have felt as familiar as the classroom to Kareem because his classroom teacher or the art, music, or gym teacher had sent him there. There were many days when his teacher and I told detailed stories to each other of what he had done, piecing together progress, trying to stay optimistic while he was driving us crazy.

Kareem was still an outsider, a Chicago ghetto kid in a basically middle-class Wisconsin school, but he was moving in on the fringes now. He sat at the same lunch table as my daughter Nora, and one day another girl was making fun of Nora's lunch, telling her it looked gross. In Kareem's tough world, you'd scarcely notice someone making fun of your lunch. But Nora took it hard, feeling embarrassed and unjustly criticized. Nora, head down, concentrated on her sandwich, bite by bite keeping the sandwich right in front of her face, as if it could be a shield to keep the other kids from seeing she was close to crying.

But Kareem saw the hurt on her face and came to her defense with a strong bark to the other girl: "Leave her alone!

She my friend!" The unfortunate kid taunting Nora backed off quickly, eyes glued on her own food.

Nora looked up at Kareem and thanked him. His response had reflected the gang rules of affiliation and altercation that Kareem at seven already knew. Nora was family to Kareem because she was my daughter. And by standing up for Nora, Kareem drew a little closer to belonging in school.

Kareem spent days and days with me in which the main struggle was keeping him on task. Three and four weeks into lessons, he still couldn't focus on one word after another. But along the way there were constant signs he was learning more. He made six attempts on the word *crocodile*—"lion-tiger-dinosaur-dinosaur-dinosaur-alligator"—each time knowing he was wrong, but not knowing how to get to what was right.

If Kareem had been reading this book in his class's reading group, he would never have had the chance to make six attempts. Other kids would have interrupted him, calling out the answer, giving him no chance to discover the word by analyzing it. Maureen Ruzicka, one of Franklin's classroom teachers, was most struck by this power of the Reading Recovery lesson after she observed one of her students with me. She said that in reading groups, children too often don't get a chance to pause at a word, to think about it, to look at the picture, to try its sound. If they pause, another child interrupts them and tells them the word. They don't get the chance to try more than one strategy on a word.

Just as important, Maureen said, the teacher doesn't get an extended chance to observe how the child tries to read difficult words. She ends up too often only seeing the surface attempt of those children who need the most intensive instruction in reading. She can teach to what she sees, but not to what the other children mute.

When Kareem tried six times to read the word *crocodile,* he was learning to draw on himself, to make another attempt if the first (or second, or third) didn't work. This is the powerful result for the child of the Reading Recovery teacher teaching by observing. There are silences when the child can think. In these silences the child learns to become independent, to draw on what he knows for other possible strategies.

In the fourteenth lesson Kareem read "Stop it" for *Stop!,* seeming to read *Stop!* as two words. Later when I had him make *stop* out of magnetic letters (*stop* had been a fluent writing word for him even before we began work together), he quickly put the four letters together correctly. Then he pulled an *i* down next to it and, looking at me slyly like he wasn't going to let me trick him, put it upside down at the end of the word. Unfamiliar with the concept of punctuation, he had interpreted the exclamation point as *it.* Then, realizing *Stop!* was one word, he regrouped and figured that he had just learned that *stop* was spelled with an upside down *i* at the end. But he had made his mistake because he had been looking closely at what he was reading. And finished with reading, the book closed, he still had a good picture in his mind of the word on the page. Kareem was learning.

We bounced back and forth between his slow but clear learning and the incessant labor of keeping him on task. Each day it was a struggle getting Kareem to my room with any semblance of order. He did flips in the halls. He hid from me behind doors, leaping out at me with a grin. Or he raced ahead of me to hide under my table, shouting "Boo!" when I entered. He wasn't really doing this to misbehave—he had misbehavior down to a malevolent art—it was because he had such incredible energy and genuinely liked me. As much as an explosion of inappropriate behavior, his actions were a dance, an offering to me. Having only a half hour a day, I decided to focus on reading and let go how he walked in the hall, rationalizing that if he released some of this energy maybe he could learn better.

But we had so much to work against. Over and over, his small vocabulary got in the way of his reading and his pride, and on the days he knew that would happen, he was very reluctant to read. Three weeks into our lessons I learned he didn't know the words *lettuce* and *tomato*—a seven-year-old boy in the United States unaware of these vegetables. I used skills I use in teaching English as a Second Language to teach Kareem because I so often had to teach him basic vocabulary.

In a similar way his proficiency in Black English got in the way of his reading. He tried five times to read *I don't want candy* because reading it comfortably in dialect he read, "I don't want no candy." Each time he finished the sentence, he knew his words didn't match. Though he didn't know how to correct his error, because he was unaware of concepts like syntax and standard and nonstandard English, he knew he had made one.

Kareem also had difficulty learning how to write and recognize high-frequency words. By our twenty-third lesson Kareem had learned to write fourteen words: *Kareem, dog, stop, no, go, I, to, a, like, the, my, there, see,* and *is.* But suddenly he started confusing them, writing *see* for *is, the* for *see.* A few days later he made a similar mistake in his reading, attempting "the-I-write-my-the" for the simple and by now well-known word *the.* I made flash cards of his fluent words, and we played a quick game each day to see how many he could read to me. Kareem felt a sense of accomplishment in reading them correctly. It was a lure that brought his attention to reading. It also was a game, and he wanted to win the game. I kept upping the stakes on how many words he would have to read correctly to beat me. He would unabashedly smile as he read, leaning forward, totally focused on the word because it mattered to win. Most children don't need this kind of incentive to become better readers, and we don't use flash cards with most Reading Recovery students. For Kareem, who was so often random and unfocused, these cards were the stretching and the pep talk before the game. They brought him to task.

I reinforced the flash cards by having him write his hard words over and over, over and over until they seemed secure. His limited writing knowledge was holding back his progress in reading. If I could tie writing to reading clearly for Kareem, and secure his fluency in both for core words (meaning he would be able to read and write the words *to, the, and, my,* and so on quickly and fluently), he would move forward in both.

But it wasn't just school and learning that were difficult for Kareem. His life was difficult, and at times it hurt. One Monday afternoon I had been working late writing reports on my Reading Recovery students. I needed a break, so I went to the school office to check my mailbox. It was three hours after classes had been dismissed, and the office would be closing soon. There was Kareem, asleep on a chair in the corner, leaning against a cabinet. The school secretary told me he had been kicked off the bus for three days for repeated behavior problems. His father had told him he would pick him up that afternoon but had never come.

Kareem woke up as we were talking, looked at me briefly and then looked down, still mostly asleep. The secretary said that the school social worker would drive Kareem home when the meeting he was in was over. I asked if Kareem could come down and wait in my room. I went over and put my arm around him and walked him out of the office.

Kareem looked ancient in his sadness. Children can be beaten down by life, and Kareem on this day was. He shrugged when I talked to him and had no words for me. This was not the usual Kareem. There was an aching in him that had had too much, and he had given up.

My reading room is quite small and has no windows. It is belowground and feels far away from everything else. Kareem worked here with me every day, and it was hard work that pushed him to his limit. As we walked in I realized how strange it must feel to him to be here so long after school. I gave him some books to look at and tried to go back to my work, but being here now clearly gave Kareem no solace. His sadness was visceral and made the dark room even darker.

I put my work aside, left a note for the social worker, and took Kareem outside. It was a gray, cold, late autumn afternoon; rain hung in the air as a thick mist. We stood near the door, sheltered by the building, and Kareem melded into the day as it fit his mood.

Kareem couldn't talk to me. He was too deep in whatever was his loss. But we were clearly here together now. I stood behind him so that we weren't looking at each other. There are times when children need the safety of not looking at you face-to-face. I told him how much I liked weather like this, how its gray stillness had always seemed to me a comfort. I pulled on memory and told him what I did in weather like this as a child.

I spoke slowly and softly, keeping my voice going as a hum for him. I did everything I could think of except ask him what was wrong. Whatever it was, it was too sorrowful right now for him to talk about. He told me that in every way he could without words. He also, by the way he slowly raised his face and eventually held onto my hands, let me know that it helped that I was with him now. But there were no words from him, no words.

The social worker found us, ready to take Kareem home. I gave him a hug and told him I'd see him the next day.

Kareem kept his distance and stayed inside himself for three days after that. Then, still so downcast, still so far away from what we think of as childhood, Kareem told me that his mother had walked out and wouldn't be back. He still had his father and five brothers and sisters. But he was a young child, and his mother was gone.

Kareem's mother had left him. And hurt and angry, Kareem left us in every way he could. He withdrew again from school and became more sullen and hostile. He swore at the bus driver, got in fights with kids, ran around the room instead of doing his work. So once again, Kareem would do so much wrong that you would have trouble believing in him and having patience with him, and then he would do something so right that you were ready to defend him against anyone.

Kareem was a regular at the free breakfast program, often eating three bowls of cereal before school because he usually was so hungry. On Fridays and Mondays he attacked the food, trying to eat as quickly and as much as possible, either to store up for the weekend or to make up for two days with little food.

There was a lot Kareem didn't have—school supplies, for example—and he went to school with other kids who were comfortable in surfeit. One morning Kareem started school standing next to his classroom teacher, waiting until he had her attention, then saying, "I found something on the bus. What should I do with it?" He held up a dollar bill and gave it to her.

The school juvenile delinquent had just been Abe Lincoln. She told him he had done the right thing and sent him to Mac McVey, our principal, so he could tell Mac what he had done and turn the dollar bill in to the office. Mac continued the praise and bought Kareem a candy bar as a reward. When I came to pick him up that morning, Kareem, at his teacher's prompting, told me the whole story, that great unabashed and embarrassed smile raised to me.

This was our moral victory, Kareem being honest when no one would have known if he wasn't. He was the Prince of Franklin that day, passed from person to person for praise, and he loved it. A note was sent home to his father, telling him about Kareem turning in the money. When I asked Kareem the next day what his father had said to him, he looked at me, eyebrows raised, kidding but not kidding all in one glance, and said, "He told me I should have kept it."

His life had the hole his mother had left, though he talked to me now about visiting her some weekends. His stomach was never full. And day after day, we continued to work on reading. I diligently had Kareem point to every word as he read, to make sure he was looking at the page, looking at the word, looking at the letters. "Did you have too many words?" "Did you have enough words?" "Does it look right?" "Does it make sense?" I popped questions at him over and over to get him to take responsibility for his own reading. I continued with the flash cards, and Kareem beat me every day. He now could identify several more core words than he could write. He read for meaning and proudly monitored initial letters. When Kareem knew he had learned a strategy, he smiled as he used it. The smile was the final stage in his acknowledging he had secured the strategy.

Finally, after Thanksgiving, the day arrived when I felt secure that Kareem had learned to monitor his reading. He had learned to look at the first letter of a word to confirm it was right and to use the core group of anchor words (now up to seventeen) that we practiced each day in the flash card game as a check on his reading. When his finger was under *is* he read "is"; when it was under *to* he read "to". At the same time, using these well-known anchor words to keep fluency, he was learning that reading is not something we do word by word, laboriously ignoring meaning.

Still reinforcing his monitoring, we moved to the next step in untangling his reading problems—helping him to focus on both the beginning and the end of a word as he checked his reading. But with a kid like Kareem, it wasn't that simple. He still would write "the" for *my* and confuse core words that hadn't been confusing one moment before. And over and over, his limited vocabulary determined, taunted, his reading. He didn't know the word *chimney* when he read, and he was visibly ashamed. The next day he tried "poundster" for *butcher* and then just shut down, unable to think of the word for who that man was.

A lot of first-graders might not know the word *butcher,* but Kareem didn't know that. He just knew that again and again he didn't know what you call things. This wasn't just reading for Kareem. His dignity was at stake as he ran up against these barriers of unknown words. He felt stupid, and I mattered to him. He didn't want to be stupid with me. He would sit, shoulders and head sinking down, as he curled into defeat. At those times he would be unable to say anything. When you are a kid who is often in trouble, you carve your dignity out of your distance, out of your disdain for rules and for the people who try to hold you to them. Kareem at that time didn't have that distance to hold on to with me. He knew

I believed in him, and I was even more important to him now that his mother had gone. It was painful for Kareem not to be able to read because he didn't know the names for things. There was a loneliness in it that I couldn't reach.

Kareem continued his slow, steady progress, reading far below his classmates but methodically putting together reading skills. By the beginning of December, he was reading books that most of our first-graders can read in September, but considering where he had started, this was significant progress. He was monitoring the beginning and the end of words and more often correcting errors as he read. You would see him, finger under each word, pausing at the first letter of the word when necessary to make sure what he read was right. He was beginning to check both meaning and what the words looked like as he read, using one system to confirm the other. It took Kareem a long time to learn a strategy, but once he did, he used it consciously and confidently. So Kareem not only used rerunning starts now, he used re-rerunning starts and re-re-rerunning starts.

And he was driving me nuts. Kareem's fidgeting and rapid darting from one thought to another, from one place to another, now had a kind of nonsense rap sound to it. He would be in the middle of reading and suddenly switch to explosive consonants, a drum roll of one right after the other: "Ch-k-b, ch-k-b, ch-ch-ch-k-ch-k-b." In seconds, he would forget the book and rock in his seat, fingers keeping rhythm on the table. I would stop what we were doing, take his face in my hands, and get him to look at me. "Kareem. Stop it. Kareem. Listen to me."

He'd look straight at me: "Ch-ch-ch-k-b." One day I stopped the entire lesson and was deadly enough that he listened. Kareem had a cousin in prison he had talked to me about, and I said to him sternly that he didn't want to end up like him. I talked about being hungry and without a home, and I told him that if he didn't want to be hungry again when he grew up he had to learn to read. He needed to read, not just to do well in school, but for his life. I would teach him as well as I could, but if he didn't act serious and try, it wouldn't matter. Kareem was quiet. Kareem was listening.

I went to the mountaintop and started my speech about Jesse Jackson. I was orating now. Did he know who Jesse Jackson was? He shook his head no. "Well, Jesse Jackson is a black leader who cares about kids, who fights for people, and who tells them to be their best and to be proud of their best. He goes around to schools and churches; he was here in Madison a few years ago, and I saw him. And one thing Jesse Jackson does when he talks to kids, to grown-ups, he gets them to say and say again, 'I am somebody.'" I was holding Kareem's head; I had him looking right at me. "I want you to say it."

"I am somebody."

"Good. Now every time you do that rap when we're working, you waste our time, and you waste your time. Say it again: 'I am somebody.'"

"I am somebody."

"You've got to believe it. You've got to believe you're worth learning to read. When you do that noise, I'm going to say, 'Kareem: I am somebody.' And I want you to say, 'I am some-

111

body' and stop the rap. I want you to pay attention. I don't want you to be hungry." The silence was all around us.

We worked on writing "I am somebody" on the board and then for his sentence that day. Kareem could write, "I smbd," which meant he heard every consonant in a three-syllable word. He took his sentence home to work on with his dad.

The next day I asked him if he had worked on the sentence. He had. Did he remember who Jesse Jackson was? Kareem looked at me knowingly and said, "Yeah, my dad's got his music tapes."

But "I am somebody" did work. From then on, when Kareem lapsed into his explosive nonsense, I would say sharply, "Kareem!" and he, repeating "I am somebody," would come back to task.

All the way through our work, Kareem was charming and impossible. I loved him, and he loved me. There was an ease between us, the unspoken comfort of people who know each other well. He also took me to my limits. Regularly in my teaching notes for Kareem I'd have comments like, "Oh, boy. Hard day."

He was now closely monitoring his reading and picking up more and more anchor words that he could check as he read, to make sure that what he was saying was actually in the book. The week before winter vacation, though we hadn't worked on writing the words *they* and *are,* he wrote them on his own for his sentence with no prompting.

Although Kareem had by now mostly backed off from his machine-gun consonants, he brought his brothers' and sisters' tapes to school in his mind. Through a lesson he'd be mumbling songs under his breath, often as unconscious of doing so as he had been of sputtering sounds. One day the subtext of our lesson was "I love you, love you, love you, baby." He sang it to me over and over all morning. But he kept making progress.

We trudged on in reading. By January, Kareem had reached the point where he usually knew if he made a mistake, although he didn't always know how to correct it. But the fact that he knew he made a mistake showed that he was now consistently cross-checking. He was checking meaning or language structure against the visual elements of words.

His written sentences were starting to have a Kareem twist to them, to sound like Kareem sounded when he talked. For example, his sentences showed Kareem's overt affection for others: "I like E.T. He is a special guy" (the underlined letters are those that Kareem wrote). Or a week later, when we read a book about a little girl named Lucy and Kareem was still under E.T.'s thrall: "I want E.T. to give Lucy a kiss."

As we worked on strategies for fixing mistakes, Kareem's first impulse was to wait me out. Perhaps if he sat long enough without saying anything, I would give in and give him the word. There were some very silent lessons, where he waited for me and I waited for him, neither of us speaking. Kareem would look up at me and try to get me to give him a clue. I would bore holes with my eyes through the word he was stuck on, refusing to respond to him.

As we went through this period, Kareem was frustrated enough with himself and with me that he tried acting out even more. One day he moved around, grabbed things, and ignored me so much when writing that I could pull only a two-word sentence from him: "H r" for "He ran." We were fighting to see if Kareem would learn more, and he didn't want to take the risk. He was too unsure, too aware of how hard things were already.

In spite of this frustration, Kareem was starting to read with expression, finding pleasure in rhyme and repetition. He sat, one hand holding the book, the other with the index finger running under the words as he read, smiling at his own certainty and his enjoyment of the gluttonous character Greedy Cat from *Greedy Cat Is Hungry* by Joy Cowley:

> Greedy Cat
> sat on a mat
> by the fridge.
> Meow, meow, meow.

Kareem had become a troubadour, a storyteller with books.

Giving kids at the bottom of the class the experience of fluency is crucial to their becoming literate. They need the experience of reading books they know how to read and expecting that they will know what the words are. They then hear themselves reading smoothly, several words in a row, instead of stumbling over one slow word at a time. With the confidence of knowing a book well, they can uncover new strategies for the few words that may still be difficult.

Too often kids at the bottom of the class don't get the chance to feel confident in reading because each time they've struggled through a book or story in a basal, they have to move on to the next one. They don't have the opportunity to really *know* a book. Or, conversely, they read and reread the same easy books but aren't challenged in instruction and given new, more difficult books at the same time.

The Reading Recovery lesson is structured to provide a careful balance of familiarity and challenge. Each day the child reads both texts that are fluent for him and texts that are difficult. Kareem began every lesson firmly in the known by spending several minutes reading books that he had read several times before. Next we took a Running Record of a book that he had read only once. Then, moving into writing, he wrote a sentence that he had just at that moment decided to write. But it was his sentence, it was one he had created and owned, so in that way it was close. Finally, the lesson ended with the introduction of a new book, a book he had never seen and now had to read with minimal help.

Kareem had now had almost a semester of instruction. Most Reading Recovery students have graduated from the program by this time, but Kareem needed much more help. It was clear that with Reading Recovery he was really learning to think about reading. Finally, he was consistently instead of sporadically correcting errors as he read, in part because he had begun to read like a reader. Until now Kareem's errors made sense and fit the syntax, but they looked nothing like the word on the page. Slowly he began to look more closely at the words, correcting "long" to "big," "nose" to "mouth."

In fact, Kareem's close monitoring of his reading had become so careful and automatic that he was now making more self-corrections than errors in his reading, the sure pay-off for the effort we had made to make certain he was looking at what he read.

We had survived the struggle to get Kareem to try harder books, and I was excited about Kareem's work now. He was showing solid progress and consistently moving into more difficult texts. His Running Records showed he was using skills we had spent months building. He was carefully attending to what he read and monitoring it to see if it looked right. He had also learned to predict text, and now he was reading what he expected to be on the page and checking as he went to see if his expectations were right. In February, I could finally say there was a fluidity to his reading.

His writing was still confused though. He regularly made errors he shouldn't have made, such as "we" for *he,* "he" for *oh.* I think he didn't care about writing the way he did about reading. Reading, unlike writing, seemed to mean security for Kareem. He felt a connection to books and deciphering them that he didn't feel with pencil and paper. In a symbolic way, writing and reading are reverse processes. Kareem seemed to like much more the discovery of reading a new book than the uncovering inherent in exposing his thoughts on paper. I came to realize that our most difficult times in the room were when Kareem was writing.

But his reading was solid now. And there was another advantage to Kareem's great progress in reading. Kareem finally felt connected to school. It was no longer an alien, suspicious place. It was a place he felt he belonged to. He was still not ready to reveal who he was at school, but he was making progress. He walked a little more slowly in the hall. He began to talk things out with the other children rather than just hit them or sullenly retreat if he felt he had been wronged. He knew that both his regular teacher and I really cared about him, and he had found his place in his classroom. He was still disruptive and could be very unfocused. But he was fitting in; he was no longer an outsider. Kids accepted him, and he accepted them.

I was proud of what he had learned, and in February I chose Kareem, my most difficult student, as the one I would take to the university to teach in front of my peers for my "Behind the Mirror" lesson. In this lesson other Reading Recovery teachers in training observe through a one-way mirror as a teacher and student go through a regular half-hour lesson.

When the last bell rang that day, Kareem, holding his coat nonchalantly over his arm, came down to my room to find me so we could leave together. He stood straighter; he felt important. He wasn't taking the bus home that day because his teacher needed him. He was very serious about the day and the task. We had trust between us, and Kareem wasn't going to mess things up for me.

At the university Kareem did his best to please me. With most students I'm wary of and discourage this close a connection. I love the kids, but I can best teach them if they are learning for themselves, not for me. But Kareem had been so disconnected from school that he needed to develop trust and relationships there first in order to feel secure enough to then learn on his own. Going to the university with me was giving him tremendous responsibility—a prelude to independence—to demonstrate his learning.

As he sat there, it seemed to matter more to him what the other teachers thought of me than of him. He didn't want to blow my reputation by acting up. He knew there were people watching us whom he couldn't see. Before the lesson began he whispered questions to me about them, unknowingly with the mike on. "Is they listening to us now?" "Can they see us?" He scooted his chair closer to mine; we were in this together.

Kareem performed for me that day, honoring what I meant to him as a teacher. He began the lesson writing "he," always a difficult word for him, on the board fluently. He eagerly read the books I gave him, curling his shoulders down to get closer to the book and physically involve himself in what he read. He read amazingly well, with 94 percent accuracy, and I know he tried his best to show what a good teacher I was. There was a real sense from Kareem that he was right in there with me on this, and I could tell he was pressuring himself. His sentence that day, pulled from the book he had just read, showed what he felt he was up against: "I can't help you." I think that's how Kareem felt that day, but he gave it his Sunday best. It was only toward the end of the lesson that I had to put my arm around him to keep him in his seat while he read.

When the lesson was over, he looked up at me expectantly to see if he had come through, if we had looked good together. I gave him a big hug, and beaming, he gave me one back.

Most of the kids I have taught like me as I like them. But my relationship with Kareem was an intense dance, more unstable. He would come close to me, let me know I really mattered to him and that he was ready to learn. Then he would pull away, shut me out and test me. He was the same with his regular teacher. He was probably able to make the phenomenal progress he did in that first-grade year because he never tested us both at the same time. When he was testing me to the limit, he was usually responding to his classroom teacher and behaving well in class. Then, when he would go through periods of acting out in class, he would settle down with me and make great progress. Through the entire year, his teacher and I told each other Kareem stories, a daily exchange for solace, humor, and solidarity. Kareem was a true example of the now well-known proverb "It takes a whole village to raise a child." He simply needed more love and expectation from school than one teacher could give. He needed us to be a village for him, not an isolated classroom.

A week after I took him to the university, we were back in hard times. Lesson seventy-nine: "Rough session today—good talk about why he has to do more on his own." Lesson eighty: "What a pistol today." Kareem was again kinetic and unconnected. He grabbed things off my desk and fidgeted with them. He didn't look at his book when he read, trying instead to start quick desultory conversations: "We going to the movies this weekend. My daddy taking us."

"Kareem, read."

He'd look at the book for another sentence.

"Hammer, man, he some righteous dude."

Kareem would then start to rap, looking at me out of the corner of his eye, knowing that he was ignoring his work. Finally in the middle of a lesson in March, I took his book from him, closed it, and told him to go back to class, because I was done trying to teach him that day. Kareem was suddenly very ready to settle down; he tried to get the book back, recited what he could from memory and begged to be allowed to stay. But I knew if I gave in, he'd learn that he could push me as far as he wanted. This lesson wasted was worth the better lessons I wanted us to have. My voice was more serious than Kareem had ever heard it.

I told him again that I was through. That I would teach him the next day, but not again that day. I finally had to walk Kareem out of the room and back into the hall. He now gave up on me and became suddenly sullen. There was a withdrawn hostility to him, buried deep inside him; he was just showing the tip. In the hall he looked deep at me, then looked away, saying nothing. This was a frightening day for both of us, and neither of us wanted to show it. He risked losing me, and once he saw that, he parried, and I risked losing him. That lesson stopped on a precipice. I didn't know if I'd get him back.

He came back the next day ready to go to college. No rap, no side remarks; he sat still in his chair and readily did whatever I said. He made only four errors in a ninety-word text, and all his errors made sense.

Kareem again started to make quick, noticeable progress. With the support of Reading Recovery he was reading now at an average basal level for first grade, phenomenal progress for a boy as kinetic as Kareem who had started so desperately behind the others. Finally, too, he was picking up a more sophisticated element of reading—the visual scanning of words. His errors showed it—"pict-pictures," "then-thin," "fate-fat," "botbom-bottom"—close approximations that just didn't make sense in context.

At the end of March, I ran into a problem that would keep getting worse until the school year ended. No one put Kareem to bed at home, and he would come to school dog tired. He would try to read with his head crooked in his arm on the table. When I told him to sit up, he would slouch over and read with a tired slur. He was in trouble in school again, picking fights with kids and ending up in the principal's office, where he would immediately fall asleep. We rocked back into ups and downs in our lessons. One day Kareem would read fluently because I had harangued him and the social worker had gone to his house, so he had slept well one night. The next day he would act out again, spinning in fatigue.

As much as I wanted Kareem's life put in order, I knew his dad, Carl, was working as hard as he could to keep the family going. In the last few months, Carl had gotten a job at a small bagel factory. He was working hard, repetitive, boring hours to keep his family together and in a house. But with Kareem's mother gone, no adult was at home after school. As the youngest, Kareem came home to swaggering teenagers who had no one to rein them in and whose approval he craved. School was not his biggest influence.

Things started tumbling together, good and bad, in our last weeks that year. I could feel the lure of the sophistication he saw in his older brothers. I could feel how much he cared about me and wanted to do well with me. I was surer and surer of Kareem's progress in reading, and more and more worried about how little sleep he was getting and how volatile he was becoming again in school.

I wrote to Kareem's dad, asking if we could arrange a time for me to come visit again so that Kareem and I could show him how much progress he had made in reading. Carl made time and wrote back right away. I had Kareem's full attention for several days as we planned what he would read and waited for the day of my visit to come.

At their house, Kareem, Carl, and I sat in the same small room I had sat in with his mother last fall. But this visit marked a culmination: in one sense it was a report, in another, a reckoning. I had Kareem read the short, fourteen-word book that had been too difficult for him when we had started lessons in the fall, to show where he had started. And then I had him read a two hundred–word book that he was confident with now. Kareem was just glowing, getting his father's attention with none of his siblings around to overshadow him.

Carl looked tired and on the edge of relaxing—for the next ten or fifteen minutes he had just this one thing to do—but he also seemed on guard because a teacher was there. He had had so many phone calls about the trouble Kareem got into that he kept waiting for the other shoe to drop with me. He gave me politeness and company manners and wariness. Then, when it seemed there really wasn't going to be anything wrong, he stopped giving me the attention he had thought he had better give me and turned to Kareem, beaming. Kareem and his dad looked each other in the eye; they had love written all over their faces. What Kareem had accomplished was tangibly there in the difference between the two books—it was the result of a lot of hard work.

I prompted Kareem to show his dad how many long words were on a page in the book he could read now. He looked goofy and important, barely speaking above a whisper as he showed his dad the pages of the hard book, thinking up things to point out. Carl enjoyed seeing Kareem shine; he playfully punched him on the arm and told him, "All right." Kareem, gleeful but embarrassed, couldn't think of anything else to say. He just sat looking down at the book, grinning.

I talked with Carl about the test that Kareem would take in about a month to see if he would graduate from the program. I told him that I thought Kareem was capable of passing the test, but he would really need to get enough sleep at home. He couldn't pay attention in school when he was so tired. Carl nodded at me seriously as I spoke. I think he knew what I was saying and felt a sense of obligation to help Kareem through. We agreed that if he could get Kareem to bed, I would do my best to get him to graduate from the program. Kareem would be really proud about that; we both wanted it for him. And Kareem would need to do his part, right, Kareem? A willing, smiling yes. I gave Kareem a hug, told him I'd see him the next day, and left.

The next day Kareem came eager to learn. He was relaxed and quiet; he clearly had slept. That day he wrote: "I love my Dad. Dad loves me reading to him, too."

But by the next week we were back with the same problems. One day when I went to get him from his class, I found him at the side of the room, dead asleep on a rug. He was so sound asleep that I couldn't wake him, so we skipped our lesson for that day. The next day he came to Reading Recovery, but he was so tired and irritable he wouldn't cooperate. Again, I sent him back to class.

If I could just teach him when he had had enough sleep, I knew Kareem would become secure in reading. We were now working on end-of-first-grade, beginning-of-second-grade trade books. When he was "on," he read confidently, checking that what he read made sense and fixing errors as he went along. Here was Kareem, a boy doomed to failure by behavior and economics, reading instructionally above grade level.

But the effects of poverty can be daily, small, and insidious. Kareem's life kept interfering with school. One day when he walked to my room with me, he tried to nonchalantly keep his hand on his knee the whole time. He walked hunched over to one side, loping instead of walking, trying to pretend he wasn't doing it. When we got to my room, he showed me that his pants had a huge hole in the knee. He was embarrassed to be wearing them and had tried to cover what caused his shame. I took him to the nurse's office for another pair of pants. After he changed and came back, he could read.

On another day his shoes were too big and had no laces; he slopped in them like an old pair of slippers. The nurse's office didn't have any shoes that fit Kareem, but I got some string, and we made it into laces.

Kareem, a boy who could run like magic, deserved better, and enough better might have kept him out of trouble. But when you looked to his father, there he was, making bagels on an assembly line, trying to keep five kids together as a family. He couldn't give them all they needed, but he was doing the best he could.

On many days my disappointment with Kareem's behavior and my frustration with how much life was against him made it sorrowful to teach him. Sometimes I felt success for him starting to spiral out of reach. And yet here he was, a poor boy who couldn't use the word *lettuce* in October reading second-grade books in May. I loved Kareem; I saw him really learning, using strategies, not rote, to read. And then I would see him acting out, acting up, not caring about school.

One afternoon one of my Hmong students told me he was afraid of Kareem, that Kareem had told him he was going to beat him up. They rode the same bus home, so that afternoon I got on the bus with them, introduced them to each other as my students. "Kareem, you know Fue. Well, he's one of my kids, and I think you'd like him if you knew him better. Fue's a great guy. I want you to get along with him."

"Fue, this is Kareem, and he's a great kid, too. You guys get to know each other."

Kareem smiled at me, willing. As I got off the bus, he kept smiling with that extra warmth Kareem could have and said, "Good-bye, Ms. O'Leary. See ya tomorrow." The next day Fue told me Kareem had been kicking Fue the whole time he was smiling at me.

As part of our training year, new Reading Recovery teachers write regular predictions of progress for our students. In these reports we try to predict how far our students will get in three weeks, documenting our predictions with what we are going to do to get them there. Throughout the year my predictions for Kareem were upbeat, hopeful, and intense. My last one was not:

> If in addition to teaching reading, I could make
> sure Kareem had enough to eat and enough sleep, that
> he had enough parent support, that someone worked

with him at home, then he would graduate from the program. But he doesn't have these things, and they are beyond my control.

And he still could succeed, but whether he does depends on how he comes to school that day.

Given all that, Kareem has developed very strong skills. He reads for meaning. He does visual analysis in the context of meaning. He self-corrects well and predicts text by structure cues. I have pulled back on book introductions and given him much more responsibility. Because of this, we are only now starting Level 14, but he is strong in what he does.

Kareem's weakness is still writing. He can only write thirty-seven words in ten minutes, and some words I thought were fluent are still not secure. He also continues to confuse *w/m, b/d*.

I will focus on writing; taking his own responsibility for how much we get done; and independence in text reading in our last weeks.

I will aim for Level 16 or 17 by the end of three weeks.

But whatever happens, I know he has learned a tremendous amount.

"But." *But* was the word for Kareem, because I could never feel one way about him. As soon as I became resigned to his not caring enough about school and accepted the inevitable, he would turn around and show that he was a sweet kid fighting heavy odds. I was out of school after a miscarriage; Kareem knew only that I was sick. Kareem T. Little, the bad boy at school, sent a note home to me through his teacher: "Der Mrs OLeary I mest you. I love you. I hop you fel bar. One day I most Fel Bad. its becs I love you. We be msing you. Love Kareem." ("Dear Mrs. O'Leary, I missed you. I love you. I hope you feel better. One day I most feel bad. It's because I love you. We be missing you. Love, Kareem.")

When I came back to school the sentences he wrote, correctly, that day were "I love you. We love us." And we did. There was an incredible warmth and acceptance between us, at times a strange equality that had nothing to do with my being his teacher, because at that level he did know that I was in charge and expected him to work. It was an equality that meant we both recognized we were close and we cared about each other. For a child like Kareem, that caring and connection had to precede his taking responsibility and becoming independent in school.

Toward the end of the school year, the school board was deciding whether or not to expand the Reading Recovery program. I was so proud of Kareem and how Reading Recovery had changed school for him that I invited the president of the school board to come observe a lesson. I thought if he saw the progress Kareem had made, how Kareem now had a chance to succeed in school, that it would help the program get better funding.

The school board president showed up. Kareem didn't. I checked the breakfast program, I checked his room, I checked the breakfast program again. Kareem, who had missed perhaps two days of school all year, and who knew I had invited someone to watch him read, simply wasn't at school. The family had no phone, so I couldn't call his home.

The president and I made polite conversation, then awkward conversation, both looking at the clock, in our different ways annoyed and disappointed. I finally got another student and started a lesson so I could at least show the president the method, show a struggling student learning to conceptualize.

And then Kareem showed up at my door. It was too late for the school board president to stay to watch a lesson with Kareem, but we found out why he had been late. Kareem had missed the bus for school, so he had run a quarter of a mile to Bayview, the low-income housing where most of our Hmong students live. But the bus had left Bayview by the time he got there. Kareem had had no breakfast, and he was hungry. But this little first-grader had walked a mile alone to school, because school was where he wanted to be.

I hugged Kareem, told him he had done the right thing, and sent him back to his regular teacher's room, telling him I'd see him later. I finished the lesson I had been in the middle of and said good-bye to the school board president. Then I went to Kareem's class and brought him back down to my room.

We both basked in pride. We sat in our kindergarten chairs next to each other, both smiling, enjoying some silence before we started the lesson. Kareem, who had trusted no one at school in September, had gone out of his way and struggled to get here in May. We both felt that we were at the end of a story, that Kareem was home. I have rarely been so proud of a child.

Kareem didn't test out of the Reading Recovery program. He came tantalizingly close, which is an apt assessment because so much about Kareem was tantalizing and just out of reach.

To successfully exit from the program at the end of the year, students need to show they can read an end-of-first-grade text at 90 percent accuracy. Kareem read it at 89 percent accuracy. With the support of a teacher, Kareem could successfully read second-grade books. But on his own he remained a hair away from what an average first-grader could read.

It takes a whole village to raise a child. Kareem needed a whole village, he needed a circle of adults committed to seeing he made it in life. But schools don't have enough adults with enough time to give kids like Kareem all they need. And their communities and families unfortunately often have less and less available for them.

The next year, not seeing me daily, Kareem was still friendly with me but, as the months passed, less and less open. He would walk by, pretending he didn't see me, looking out of the corner of his eye at me. If I said something, he would turn back and smile at me, or come back for a hug, by now willing to open up. But we never had much time together, and the opening up didn't go far enough.

In second grade Kareem continued to be in and out of trouble. Without the lure of daily one-on-one attention, he wasn't as motivated to do well. His father got tired of hearing that Kareem was in trouble at school and lost interest in working with Kareem on discipline. Kareem's regular teacher was thus often left very alone in trying to keep him learning and being his best. Because his best was still out there for us. Kareem's best was always charming, always sincere and affectionate, always full. But it was hard for him to keep it up; the lure away was much stronger.

There was a story people told about Kareem in second grade. The enrichment teacher was in Kareem's class in December, and her focus that week was on Norway and winter celebrations. She talked about Saint Lucia, about rosemaling, different things that could help young children see and imagine a culture. Then she played a song in Norwegian that she described to us as Ray Coniff corny—overarranged with cheery voices. Kareem was sitting next to his friend Ben, a white kid who couldn't possibly look any more college-bound white. Tortoiseshell glasses falling off his nose, ingenuous and gawky. Kareem listened to the music a bit, then turned seriously to Ben and said, "That be your kind of rap?"

His question gives a clue as to how "white" and foreign school can be for minority kids. I suppose in a way a lot of our good intentions sound like the Ray Coniff singers to a boy who has seen what Kareem has. But it also gives a clue as to how innocent and willing to believe kids still are at Kareem's age. This stuff sounded pretty weird to him, but he was willing to believe it was a cultural thing and make the analogy that this was repressed, white bread rap. School may have been like coming to Mars for Kareem, but he was doing his best to make sense of it.

There were always two Kareems. The boy of sweet innocence and goodness, the one who loved so willingly and showed real potential, even with all his problems. And then the cocky boy-man of eight, who felt the lure of being separate, of pulling back, of affirming his distance from school and expectation. This Kareem brashly drew gang insignia on his hand in second grade. This Kareem still loved love and affection but had learned not to trust it.

When Kareem started third grade, his brother was expelled from middle school for bringing a gun to school. When I heard that news, my heart sank; the odds against Kareem seemed impossible. But I keep the following in front of me, too: Kareem has a father who didn't leave. Kareem has an essential goodness that led him to return money he found on the bus and to walk to school alone and hungry rather than miss a day. And Kareem can read.

Nkauj Hli
Daughter of Refugees

I remember seeing Nkauj Hli in kindergarten, before I taught her or knew her. Her class would file past in a long line, moving from one room to another. The children were quiet and serious (mostly) about this civilizing task of getting somewhere together, the tops of their heads making a straight line as they walked past. Until the line got to Nkauj Hli. She would be somewhere in the middle of the line, resigned to standing out, a good eight inches taller than any other child in her class. After Nkauj Hli the line went back down eight inches and continued straight as the class moved on. If you watched the line until it disappeared, the last thing you saw was Nkauj Hli's head and shoulders, moving on, floating above all else.

The Hmong are in general a smaller people than most Americans, so it was unusual that she was taller than the other children. She was also heavy, again not the norm for young Hmong children. But despite her size, she was not ungainly. Nkauj Hli revealed grace and sorrow in how she moved without words, for she knew she didn't fit in.

Her mother was a pretty woman, as was her older sister, Xue. Xue was a complex girl, caught between two cultures. Already at seven, you could tell she wanted to assimilate into American culture. She was a good kid but unusual for a Hmong girl in that she sought out white girls to play with at school, instead of the girls from her neighborhood. Xue was going to get out of what was around her.

Nkauj Hli, towering over Xue, lived in her shadow. Their mother taught Hmong dances to Xue and her pretty cousin, Mai Choua. She sewed beautiful Hmong holiday clothing for them, and they danced at festivals and for children at school. They were mesmerizing in their serious, silent gestures and vibrant Hmong colors and detail. Nkauj Hli watched them with the rest of us, judging herself for not being pretty like Xue.

Nkauj Hli didn't understand school, but she acceded to it. Hmong children are quiet; Nkauj Hli was quieter. She carried a burden that she didn't know she showed. She failed but didn't want to. Resignation was simply the softest response.

When I began working with Nkauj Hli in January of first grade, most of what I knew of her was her look, which I had seen now for a year and a half. She was at the bottom of her class because she was so reluctant to make a mistake, to speak up. She had become accustomed to and comfortable in silence. But both her English as a Second Language teacher and her classroom teacher said she was ready to blossom. Her reading skills were low, but the things she could do silently showed real progress from the beginning of the year. Nkauj Hli could comfortably read only short patterned sentences in January. But she could write twenty-eight words in ten minutes and read them back in a serious whisper. She had taken in as much as she could without drawing attention to herself.

Another thing I noticed about Nkauj Hli—in a year in school, Nkauj Hli had learned to stoop. In kindergarten she had towered above the other kids but had been resigned to it. By first grade she had started to pull herself in and to hunch her shoulders and her head, trying to be less of herself so people wouldn't notice her.

In the early 1980s, when I started teaching Hmong children, most of them were refugees who had been born in Laos at the end of the Vietnam War or born later in Thailand in the refugee camps.

The Hmong are a montagnard people who for centuries lived separate from other Asian cultures. At the end of the nineteenth century they fled persecution in China and settled primarily in the mountains of Laos but spilled, too, over borders into Cambodia and Vietnam. They are a proud people with a strong sense of family, duty, and right and wrong. In Southeast Asia they lived in clans, with elders who settled disputes and had final say over people's lives. Members of this agrarian slash-and-burn culture had more in common with people in early medieval Europe than in the late-twentieth-century United States. Culture shock is a very mild phrase to describe what the Hmong have gone through in moving to the quick life, materialism, and freedom of postmodern United States.

Hmong women's lives in Laos seem repressively restricted to an American woman. The traditional ceremony around marriage was for the woman to be kidnapped from her family and taken off by the man. Often, under the surface, both the families and the woman knew the kidnapping would take place. The kidnapping was a form that was representative of deeper roles instilled in Hmong society.

But women were also kidnapped against their will and, damaged goods after the kidnapping, forced to become a part of and bear children in a clan they hadn't chosen. Young Hmong women in the United States have begun to question this custom. I knew one gutsy, determined young Hmong woman who reached her teens in the United States. She was kidnapped by three different men but escaped each time. Once she jumped from a car, once from the window of the second-story room she had been locked in. Sufficiently Americanized, she refused a custom that so determined her life; she would not be owned.

There is also a beauty in Hmong culture that stands out as boldly as the kidnapping—the needlework, or *pandau,* that Hmong women create. *Pandau* is the name for both Hmong embroidery and reverse appliqué. The reverse appliqué is made from such thin strips of fabric, concentrically repeating a design, that only an incredibly skilled American needle artist would even attempt it. In old Hmong culture this needle craft was a skill that almost all women eventually learned. It shows a way of seeing the world that is not modern American. It recognizes rhythm and interrelatedness and the beauty of repetition. The designs are symbolic of nature—the elephant's foot, the snail, even the path from death to the spirit world. I see a Hmong mother's relationship to her children in the spirals of *pandau;* there is a matter-of-fact connectedness and continuity between the Hmong generations that is reflected in their visual arts.

What drew me to learning more about the Hmong was that until fifty years ago there was no written language for Hmong. Hmong and its traditions were oral, handed down in spoken ceremony. The Hmong sense of speaking is thus different from ours, in that is the primary means of passing on history and preserving spoken language culture.

On the other hand, written language, though it now has preserved Hmong stories and traditions, is new, is foreign, and is not truly Hmong. Because it was developed by French missionaries, Hmong is written in the modern European alphabet, with the same letters we use in English and not in an Asian orthography.

Written Hmong looks strange to English speakers because letters appear and mix where they don't seem to belong. It is a tonal language, with meaning conveyed by nine registers that English speakers find difficult even to hear, let alone to differentiate. The missionaries marked these tones in writing by putting unspoken consonants at the end of words, each representing a different tone. *B, j, m,* and *v* can all come at the end of a word, but they aren't spoken. The boy's name Ntshiab (the *n* and *t* signal an unvoiced stop) is pronounced "chee-ah" in English. Fwm is "fue." The pronuciation of Nkauj Hli has been Americanized to "go lee."

It is not only the Hmong sense of language and sound that is different from ours. The Hmong sense of time is different, too. Though most Hmong had some education in the Lao language in Lao schools and so had contact with more ordered time, there aren't months and weeks in Hmong the way we know them. There are moons and the changes of season. Most older Hmong don't know the specific day they were born or even the year, because it simply didn't matter. They were born and taken care of, and they soon learned to take care of family and clan.

Verb tenses in Hmong show how different Hmong time is from Western time. There are only two tenses—"now" and "ago." "Ago-ness" isn't shown by adding an auxiliary or changing the ending of a verb as in English. Instead a number is said early in the sentence to show just how much "ago" is implied.

Similarly, the endings of verbs don't change to show singular or plural or first, second, or third person. A highly complex set of nouns showing relationships among people (e.g., elder sister, mother's first cousin) carries these meanings, not the verb. Thus, just as any English speaker learning a romance language has problems with feminine and masculine nouns (is it *le fromage* or *la fromage?*), Hmong speakers learning English have problems with plural forms and learning to voice verb endings. But along with grammar, the differences in language also show a difference in time and a difference in relationships. If the past is depicted as "ago-ness," it is more spatial and can be vaguer. And if nouns constantly show relationship and connectedness, the language gives a sense of community, of interdependence, that we don't have in English.

The stories the refugee children told me of their lives describe a very different time and place. One boy I taught remembered his father shooting a tiger ready to pounce at them from a tree they had been sleeping under in the forest. Two boys, cousins, remembered playing together in a river running through the main refugee camp in Thailand. These were the vaguest memories of early childhood, the kind of memories that feel like they are slipping away as we speak but hover, ephemeral. The boys would have been two or three at the time, and they couldn't tell me much more than the feeling of water, the look of the land, but they laughed as they spoke, catching each other's eye, surprised to have the same remembrance.

Another girl, who lived in a refugee camp until she was five and then moved to Madison, remembered watching a younger sister die in the camp because there was no medicine for her. She was matter-of-fact as she described her sister and her sister's death to me; this was simply part of life. She kept this one strong image that she could describe well—her little sister toddling on a dusty path. That was how she still saw her.

The children I teach now have generally been born in this country, but they, too, live between cultures. If they are younger children in a family, they grow up with older siblings speaking mostly English and parents speaking Hmong. Often their parents, especially the mothers, are illiterate, or more specifically aliterate, since Hmong is only recently a written language, and most of the parents who grew up in Laos would have had little reason to learn it.

The older parents, those who came of age in Laos, see their children slipping away to American culture, becoming disrespectful and rejecting what has always been the Hmong way. But even as they worry about losing their children, the Hmong women have a possibility of freedom that was unimaginable in their lives in Laos. You see the women of all ages enjoying this.

The younger parents have usually had at least some high school in the United States and have seen but not caught the brass ring. They want the material ease American culture promises, but they also want the familial sureness of Hmong culture. The parents of most of the children I teach live in poverty but know there is more. They speak Hmong with their children at home and take courses hoping for more sureness in English, for a better job. The TV is generally on, the shades are usually pulled, and it is not uncommon for ten people from three generations to live in one small, low-income apartment.

This is the world Nkauj Hli left each day—a world between cultures, in flux and contradiction—to come to a school where she did her best to be polite and invisible. She was a contained presence. She didn't volunteer; she didn't move unless she had to.

To teach Nkauj Hli to read well in just a few months, I had to help her lower her barriers and be more fully with me. She had to become comfortable enough to take risks. I first reached her by being quiet with her and smiling at her. ESL children learn to pick up nonverbal cues to read people and situations. In not speaking much, but showing her a real ease and pleasure in being with her, I could let her know I saw her. She had become so invisible that aside from the teachers she knew well few people paid her any attention. My smiling every day, specifically at her, helped Nkauj Hli feel comfortable with me, feel that she was there. She was sweet and innocent and an easy child to care about. But she was not the kind of child who gets a lot of recognition in any class, because she didn't ask for it and she didn't cause problems. It was new for Nkauj Hli to have someone repeatedly focus on her alone.

Roaming Around the Known was a crucial time for Nkauj Hli, because she had thought she knew very little. Spending two weeks on the same books and words allowed her to relax and to try things on her own. Each day there was a little more of Nkauj Hli there—the beginning of a smile, a moment when her eyes would look into mine and then quickly look down.

ESL children often read approximately two years below grade level, and this lag in reading, more than anything else, puts them at the bottom of the class. Teaching most ESL children to read well in first and second grade is difficult because the children just aren't proficient enough in English, the language they are trying to learn how to decode. But it can be done, and it changes a child's life.

I have learned that how you talk to kids about words establishes how they see themselves in learning. If you ask a bilingual child, "Do you know what this is?" and they don't know the word for an object in English, their easiest response is "No," which makes them feel they don't know things. If you ask instead, "What do you call this in your language?" the child can often answer. I repeat their answer and then say, "In English we call it _____." This approach allows a reciprocity between us. The child feels competent, learns more quickly, and, again, feels seen.

In teaching ESL students to read, it is crucial to understand in what ways a limited vocabulary is their major barrier to learning to read. Not knowing a word in English doesn't mean they don't understand the concept it represents—there is a difference between words and things.

Letters are symbols for sounds, and words are symbols for things. ESL children learn two sets of symbols at the same time they learn to decode each. Most of our ESL students have a good knowledge of letters and sounds by the time they are halfway through first grade. We then teach them unknown symbols—English words—through their known symbols of letters and sounds and through the general meaning they can infer without total fluency. It takes patience and respect for the child in facing this difficult task.

Most children learn to read by bringing meaning through the front door to decoding. They decode words while they know what they are reading about. ESL children have to come through the back door, learning to apply decoding so that they can get to a specific meaning and figure out a new word by context.

In our first days in Roaming, Nkauj Hli and I read *What's Inside? The Alphabet Book* by Satoshi Kitamura, an ABC book with fanciful pictures. On the first day Nkauj Hli couldn't find three objects—a guitar, a hippo, and a ladder—in the illustrations because she didn't know the words for them in English.

With *ladder,* we were on the *L* page, and she knew the letter's name and could read it. A ladder was clearly central in the picture, but she didn't know the name of that object in English, although she knew that the thing leaning against the tree was probably what she was supposed to name. I asked her what she would call this thing in Hmong and told her the English word, and we kept reading. After a few days *ladder, guitar,* and *hippo* were part of her vocabulary. Often ESL students are taught English and then given books to read. With Nkauj Hli we turned the process around, and she ended up much further ahead in school, learning to read and becoming much more fluent in English. She also was learning, by voicing what she knew, to take risks.

We wrote an "I Like" book, with sentences about things Nkauj Hli liked to do. By not speaking but drawing and writing simple sentences, Nkauj Hli could show me more about herself. On the fourth day Nkauj Hli wrote "I like to play" and drew herself, a little M. B. Goffstein person, at a chalkboard playing school. I asked her to write whatever she wanted on the board, and with delicate control she wrote in very small letters, "A B C."

Nkauj Hli's picture of herself playing, where favorite play meant playing school, showed how much she wanted to learn. She told me in a soft, low voice that she taught her younger sister and brother at home, and they were learning their ABCs. The picture helped her describe herself not as someone at the bottom of her class but as a teacher, someone who could help other children learn. As Nkauj Hli began to reveal herself, we slowly changed how she saw herself.

It is hard to learn *in* a language as you learn the language itself. One of the reasons Nkauj Hli was so unsure of herself is that until they become fluent in English, bilingual children are usually a beat behind native English speakers in figuring out what is going on in class. A common long stage in acquiring a second language is spent continually and rapidly translating back and forth between the native language and the language being learned. The child hears directions from the teacher, quickly translates them into her native language to be able to understand them, and then goes back to listen to more English.

But in that beat when the child was making sure she understood, the teacher has continued on with other instructions, and the child hasn't fully heard them. Consequently, ESL children are then only partially sure they are doing what they've been told to do. They don't want to ask the teacher each day to repeat what she said. So they spend most of their time in school uncertain about themselves and about school. It has to be a difficult way to learn, and it robs them of a confidence they would have if they were learning in their own language. What is most destructive to the students is that it subliminally teaches them that if they don't understand what they are supposed to do, they must not be very smart. The repetition of doing the same kind of task over and over for two weeks in Roaming gave Nkauj Hli sureness. She now was tentatively seeing herself as capable and even inquisitive.

By our fifth Roaming session Nkauj Hli had four books she could read well. She spoke and responded little aside from when she read, but on this day when I asked her to choose books to read, she went right away for the hardest ones and read them first. From then on, she always tried the most difficult things first. For a silent girl at the bottom of the class, the gesture of reaching for hard books spoke to how she was changing her image of herself. And she knew now that she was also telling me about herself.

In our seventh Roaming session, after I praised her for how well she was doing, Nkauj Hli immediately chose her next book: *I Can Read* by Margaret Malcolm. She read the self-affirming phrases over and over:

I can read to Mom.
I can read to Dad.
I can read to Nana.
I can read to my sister.
I can read to my teacher.
I can read to my friend.
I can read to myself.

Books were our link. They provided Nkauj Hli the opportunity to speak without using her own words. She used books to show me how well she could be the dutiful daughter.

After two weeks of unstructured Roaming sessions, Nkauj Hli trusted me and was ready to move on in reading. Each day when I came to get her, she would be sitting properly and silently at her desk. Lips tight together, face unmoving, her eyes would come up to mine as she said nothing but carefully and neatly put away pencil and paper and walked over to me, putting out her hand for me to take. As we walked to my

145

room, I would talk to her. She was mostly silent, her eyes straight ahead. But her hand was securely in mine.

We began formal lessons, and in those first few days we focused on the most common mistake Hmong children make when first reading—not pronouncing the letter *s* at the end of a word. Most Hmong children, used to the intricacies of a tonal language that doesn't use plural markers as we do, simply don't hear the final *s* in English, and so they don't pronounce it. As they read beginning books, they continually drop it.

In Nkauj Hli's first formal lesson, she made eleven errors in her Running Record of a little book with fifty-eight words. On the surface this meant the book was much too hard for her, but an analysis of her errors showed how well Nkauj Hli was actually reading. Nine of the errors came from dropping the final *s;* the other two errors reflected words she didn't know in English: *hay* and *polar.* (She did successfully read *hippo,* a word that hadn't been in her vocabulary two weeks before.)

I modeled pronouncing the final *s* for her. Within a few days she understood that it was an important skill for her to work on. In pronouncing the final *s,* she heard herself read and speak more fluently, sounding like a native English speaker. Even more important, in monitoring that she was reading the final *s,* Nkauj Hli was learning to look closely at words as she read.

That first lesson of Nkauj Hli's was at the end of January. Though her reading was far behind that of her classmates, her writing showed how much she had already learned about words and sounds. She wrote (the letters she wrote on her own are underlined): "Monkeys eat bananas. So do gorillas." In

two sentences with twenty-six sounds, she heard and correctly wrote all but six. This was excellent writing for a struggling
student at the end of January, and it showed that Nkauj Hli had
writing skills she could learn to transfer to reading. Nkauj Hli's
writing also showed the sincerity and purposiveness with
which she always learned. She had just read a book where her
main error was dropping the final *s*. Once I pointed this out to
her, she wanted to learn not to do it. Immediately she worked
on hearing the *s* at the end of *monkeys* and *gorillas*. Again, it
is hard for native Hmong speakers to hear and say the final *s*.
To work on hearing and saying (and writing) that *s*, Nkauj Hli
had to go beyond a way of knowing and seeing that was
secure to her.

But she did, because Nkauj Hli knew this time was a gift to
her. Alone, away from other students' attention, the calm,
inquisitive part of who she was could risk surfacing from her
shyness. Nkauj Hli felt me guiding her, which made her feel
safe. But it was her will and desire that took my explanations
and focus and turned her into a fluent, successful reader.
Whenever I spoke to her, she would watch me silently with a
serious, attentive expression, not moving, as if her stillness
would help her take in more.

As we progressed through the early lessons, Nkauj Hli
gave herself with devotion to whatever I focused on. By lesson three she read every final *s*, a remarkably quick mastery of
a difficult English concept for speakers of Hmong.

As we finished with the simplest books, Nkauj Hli's errors
were almost solely on words she didn't know in English: *vine,
trick, menu, supermarket*. She was reading fluently, trying to

make what she said sound like talk. In the book *No, No* (The Wright Group), her soft, sweet voice was now finally heard as she assumed the persona of different characters:

Bug, come and talk to me.
No, no. A bird is after me.

Bird, come and talk to me.
No, no. A cat is after me.

Cat, come and talk to me.
No, no. A dog is after me.

These little books allowed Nkauj Hli to speak up in school and find her voice. As she read more, she read better, becoming used to the sound of her voice. And always, after reading a book for her Running Record, Nkauj Hli would turn to me, silent, her eyes on mine, watching me for instruction. She knew this was a time in the lesson to consciously learn new things.

Nkauj Hli loved coming to reading. For a child who had felt so isolated and awkward, the recognition I gave her and the trust between us was helping her learn to read. But she now needed to learn to go beyond me. The next thing I had to teach her was not to turn to me for help in difficult tasks but to rely on herself. At the same time, I did not want to diminish her trust in me or her connection to school. Nkauj Hli had begun to sit and wait for me to help her when she came to unknown words because she hadn't yet developed the skills to figure them out. I now needed to break her of this habit and help her learn to try unknown words on her own.

In learning to read, children learn to juggle thinking about meaning while looking at and analyzing words. They unconsciously use the structure of language as word following word becomes more fluent; they begin to predict what would be the likely next word before they even look at it.

Because Nkauj Hli wasn't comfortable in English, she couldn't yet use this kind of prediction to become more fluent in reading. So to get her to try unknown words, I focused first on having her slowly stretch out the words as she read, a skill she already used well in writing.

But writing and reading use different order in meaning. In writing, the word is first in our head and then on the paper. In reading, it is first on the paper and then in our head. When she wrote, Nkauj Hli could stretch out words that she knew and hear their sounds. But in reading, it is a different skill to *find* the sound by stretching out the letters you see until they perhaps make sense (you may not know the meaning of the word even if you can pronounce it correctly).

But Nkauj Hli worked on it, and she was such a serious learner that whatever skill she was working on slowly transformed itself into a higher-level skill. She monitored for final *s* and began to read with more expression. She monitored for letters in order across unknown words and began to confirm for meaning, making nonsense errors but then correcting them as she read. This confirming of meaning meant that Nkauj Hli was learning to make sure that what she said made sense—the essential skill in becoming a fluent reader.

Nkauj Hli drank me in when we were together. She had four younger brothers and sisters, so aside from time with her grandmother, whom she visited regularly after school, Nkauj Hli had probably rarely had a repeated opportunity like this for undivided adult attention. And that repeated, sure attention was what would enable her to learn.

Trusting now that I would listen, she began a litany with me as we walked to my room together that was much like the sentences in one of the first books she saw as success, *I Can Read*. She would name the children in her family she had read to the previous night: "I read to Pa Dawb, and to Tooj, and to Ntxawg, and to Xue." She had gained more confidence in English, and her voice would go up at the end of each brother's or sister's name as she sang me her well-done homework. Nkauj Hli was the dutiful child, finally succeeding. She hadn't imagined she could do this in school.

She started to talk to me now about other children at school. Each day I taught Reading Recovery to another Hmong girl in her class, Jenna. She had been just as shy as Nkauj Hli but now was a magpie.

Nkauj Hli admired her and hoped to have her as a friend. As we walked to my room now, she would tell me what Jenna had done that day, if she had played with Jenna on the playground, and what Jenna had said. Jenna was oblivious to Nkauj Hli's feelings and never really became a good friend. But in reaching out and admitting her hopes about Jenna to me, Nkauj Hli was more fully connected to school. She was starting now to search other people out, to give up the sureness of being invisibly alone. And with this connection, Nkauj Hli now thought that she could learn.

Her increasing confidence showed in the type of refined and meaningful errors in reading that she made and carefully corrected. She read "come" for *came* and then correctly read "came." For *tent,* a word not in her English vocabulary, she read "teent," an excellent attempt.

We were now at lesson fourteen, after almost three weeks of daily instruction. As children start to get an idea of what reading is, they begin to see parts of words as a whole instead of looking at them letter by letter. Nkauj Hli began to show that she was doing this, reading *behind* as two parts: "be-hind." She was stymied by the word *caught* because that irregular past tense wasn't in her vocabulary (and how would you phonetically read *caught?*). After pausing, she read it as "catch," an excellent error that showed she was thinking about meaning as she read.

Nkauj Hli was even starting to use syntax coupled with meaning in her predictions of what a word would be. We read *The Lion's Tail,* a folktale in which a lion can't find his tail and a turtle helps him realize he is sitting on it. Nkauj Hli read:

"Why are you cry-sad?" [self-correcting for *sad*]
"I can't find my tail."
"Well-I'll help you find it." [self-correcting for *I'll*]

I was excited by these errors, for they showed that Nkauj Hli was becoming fluent and comfortable in English and in reading. In the corresponding illustration, the lion was crying, so to begin to say *cry* was an excellent prediction of what word would make sense next in the sentence. *Well* looks similar to *I'll*, and people often begin a sentence with *well* when speaking. What's more, after making each error, she corrected it, which showed that Nkauj Hli was looking closely at the page.

Her writing also was growing more fluent and easy. That day she wrote, "I <u>bet</u> I <u>can</u> <u>find</u> <u>your</u> <u>tail</u>," hearing every sound in order as she wrote.

At the same time, now working on harder skills, Nkauj Hli went back to dropping the final *s* when she read. This "learning and losing" is common as the skill of reading is acquired, and when I brought her attention to it, she quickly returned to paying attention to that difficulty in English.

But she continued to wait for me to tell her words when she read. Nkauj Hli had learned to be patient, so she could easily wait me out. After the Running Record we continued to work on slowly stretching unknown words so that sound followed sound without any pause, so that there was a rhythm to her eye and her voice moving together across the words: "L…ea…ve… s." "P…o…n…d." We practiced difficult words each day so that the technique of stretching words became familiar.

In every other way Nkauj Hli was showing tremendous growth in reading. Most of her errors involved medial vowels, the last element children generally are aware of in a word. She read "grew" for *grow* and then hit a few difficult days trying to sort out the meanings and pronunciations of *where, were,* and *are.*

Nkauj Hli was following a usual path of children learning to read in having trouble now with vowels. But gaining control of middle vowels was made more difficult for her because she was learning to read them not in her native language but in her "school" language. In isolation, *where* and *were* sound awfully similar. I found that Nkauj Hli didn't understand that *were* is the past tense of *are*. Until she did, it was a meaningless word for her. Trying "where," which had meaning for her, was actually a good guess for *were*.

She worked *where, were,* and *are* out and the next day read a book with the confusing words *hear, heard,* and *hard. Hear* and *heard* are written almost exactly alike but don't sound alike. *Heard* and *hard,* said with a midwestern pronunciation, sound similar, especially to someone just learning the language.

As we worked on visual analysis and arcane meanings, Nkauj Hli haltingly started trying to say unknown words. In lesson thirty-two she read the word *sort* correctly, then sat patiently waiting until I, too, finally said the word, letting her know she was right. In the next sentence she read *might* and again stopped, unsure of herself. But this was progress. She was now making an attempt before she stopped reading. *How* she read as "now," *lots* as "lost." Nkauj Hli's errors reflected whole words that were visually similar to the correct words.

We moved to the part of reading that simply involves believing in yourself. I talked to Nkauj Hli about how often she said a word right but didn't trust her attempt. I told her not to wait for me when she read and that I wasn't going to help her when she stopped. I wanted her to continue right ahead after trying a word. Nkauj Hli looked at me seriously. She was ready now to do anything I asked, even be independent.

Nkauj Hli's silent awareness of words continued to grow as her reading improved. In lesson thirty-four she wrote about a boy and a dog in a story:"I choose you because you choose me." In lesson thirty-six she wrote, "We swapped socks but it didn't work." Writing words like *didn't* and *choose* independently is a high-level skill for any first-grader. But Nkauj Hli had learned to look at words and remember them. Now that her reading and writing skills were closer together, she was able to make solid, accelerated progress. Even with second language interference, she was able to read books easily.

She also was becoming a different child, still quiet and gentle, but with an ease that showed she was less afraid, less an outsider. She had first risked being seen. Now she was risking change. Instead of waiting for me to teach, she now asked questions. Her voice was fuller, more sure, and she looked up at me as she spoke. When we walked to my room, she still put her hand out to hold mine as we walked. But the way she held it was more confident, more as someone giving, not just receiving. Nkauj Hli had spent a year and a half trying to withdraw and become invisible. As she felt more a part of school and risked more, her face revealed a new softness. It showed the sweet girl she had been protecting.

Her errors now showed how much children read using meaning, not just the visible elements of words. She was confused by the expression "I hate it when" because she thought the girl in the story was saying she hated her sister. That was just too mean to Nkauj Hli, and she stopped, bewildered. Later in the story, the word *climb* was difficult because of its irregular spelling. She hesitated and then read "come-b," which showed she was thinking about meaning and structure and was trying to incorporate that strange final *b* into what she said.

A few lessons later she made a similar good-sense error, reading "brangt" for *brought*. Nkauj Hli probably didn't remember the past tense for *bring* but had an idea it was irregular, so she tried "brang" in analogy with *sing/sang*. But she couldn't just say "brang" because she noticed the *t* at the end. With "brangt" she brought together meaning, structure, and the visual part of the word.

By the middle of April she was consistently using language structure in her prediction of words—a strong and unusual skill for an ESL student to rely on. From now on, though the books got progressively harder, every book but one was easy for Nkauj Hli. That was a book I didn't choose well, a book about airports. It had too much unknown vocabulary for her, and trying to read and make sense out of new words like *suitcases, cargo, the hold, fuel*, and *control tower* simply overpowered her. It was a good lesson for me in carefully matching the book to the child. But, conversely, her doing poorly on this book also showed just how well she had learned to read for meaning. Once meaning disappeared, her ability to read well did, too. This meant Nkauj Hli had learned not just to decode but to read.

The last weeks of Nkauj Hli's lessons showed how much she had internalized about reading and writing, and how much not being a native speaker of English was all that kept her from reading far above grade level.

In May she wrote, accurately, a sentence about the fable *The Ant and the Dove:* "He pointed his gun at the dove." To write this sentence, she consciously generated words: *his* from *is, gun* from *fun, dove* from *love.* Knowing she could generate words helped Nkauj Hli feel very confident about her writing.

In lesson fifty-four the only reading errors she made were tense based—"run" for *ran,* "bite" for *bit,* and, most interesting, "helpted" for *helped.* Nkauj Hli knew the *-ed* chunk meant past tense, and she knew it was pronounced "ed" as in *wanted.* She hadn't consciously taken in that many *-ed* words are pronounced with a "t" sound instead of "ed" at the end. But she had unconsciously internalized that fact because she pronounced *helped* correctly as "helpt." Her voiced addition of "ed" for the past tense meant she saw the *-ed* on the end. Nkauj Hli knew both the sound and the meaning of *-ed;* she just hadn't merged those into one yet.

In her very last lessons Nkauj Hli's rare errors were generally on unknown words, and she had learned well to try to bring meaning to reading difficult words. She read "auncles" for *Aunty*—showing that she had started to read the word visually and knew that aunts were like uncles, but she couldn't quite remember the word for the woman. But the meaning was clear in what she read. This kind of error boded well for Nkauj Hli's future success in reading because it showed it mattered to her to make sense as she read.

When I had started to work with Nkauj Hli at the end of January, she could barely read a book with a pattern that most first-graders read in September or October:

The girl looks at the bear.
The boy looks at the bear.
Can you find the bear?

When we finished lessons less than four months later, she was successfully reading texts written for the end of second grade. When she tested out of Reading Recovery, the last story she read began, "Once upon a time a man and a dog were each other's friend. They hunted together and they shared each other's food."

In January she could successfully write twenty-eight words in ten minutes. Now she could write fifty-eight. In January she could write twenty-seven out of thirty-seven sounds in a dictation. When given the end-of-the-year dictation to write, she heard and wrote all thirty-seven sounds, a phenomenal increase for a child learning to discriminate vowel sounds in a language that sounded little like her own.

Nkauj Hli's first-grade test scores showed a child who had made great progress in school. Her face showed a child who had been transformed. Nkauj Hli's sorrow had disappeared. She smiled now, easily, and her smile was beatific. The grace Nkauj Hli had unknowlingly carried showed in the ease she was beginning to feel. Nkauj Hli was still on the fringes of Franklin and still didn't mingle with many other kids, but she now felt she had a place here. She now felt that this was *her* school, where she came to learn.

Nkauj Hli's journey outward from invisibility and defeat was much like the concentric images of *pandau* cloth. The beauty of *pandau* is in its silence and its repetition. Shapes flow out like the afterimage of a stone thrown in water. As Nkauj Hli risked the rhythm of coming out and of being seen, she risked being more vulnerable, more open, more simply "there." Once she knew she was seen, she grew, she changed, she became more of herself. But this more confident Nkauj Hli was still the effect, the reflection, of the stone thrown in the beginning. There was always a silent integrity to Nkauj Hli that came from the core of a child once graceful in the defeat of not fitting in.

In our early days together, when Nkauj Hli first dared to look at me but not to speak, her eyes carried the assumption that whatever she did would be wrong. She was afraid to try things because she hated to fail—and she knew all she would do was fail. Now having known success, Nkauj Hli asked questions because she wanted to learn. She attentively listened to everything I said because she knew it would help her in school. The resignation she had felt before had changed to sure patience and reflection.

There are a few children who truly love books, and even the way they carry them shows this. Nkauj Hli became one of those children. She held books close to her, making them her own, cradling them, loving them. She spent second grade almost as silent as before, but now she wrote reams and read whatever and whenever she could. When Nkauj Hli read for me at the end of second grade, she was reading fifth-grade books. By the end of third grade, she confidently and easily read a selection from a seventh-grade reader.

In Reading Recovery, Nkauj Hli learned to read and learned to hold books close because they were magic. She also learned to hold herself differently. By the end of first grade Nkauj Hli no longer stooped. She stood tall, still taller and larger than the other kids, but now she believed in herself. She still moved so gently that she appeared to float. But now it was as a girl secure in the shelter of learning, holding onto a book.

Rebekka
The Failing Poet

Cornrows, line after line, repeating across her head. Rebekka's mother, Jamaica, spent hours with her daughter seated in her lap, again and again dividing Rebekka's hair into three strands, taking up more from this side, taking up more from that, and then weaving them slowly, over and under, over and under, until all of Rebekka's hair had been braided exactly, close to her scalp. Not a wisp out of place. Love, time, and order all neatly imposed. Imposed by Jamaica as much for herself as for her daughter.

Rebekka was the fourth of four children. They had three different fathers and three different last names. Only Rebekka's father, Bobby, was still around. He came up from Illinois to see them fairly regularly. A construction worker, he had been laid off for a year now, and houses were still not being built.

Jamaica's mission in life was to raise her children so that they were safe and upright. Her own childhood had been nothing like that. Her mother was an alcoholic who disappeared when Jamaica was eleven. For a few years Jamaica had pretended at school that she still had a mother at home, and she talked about her enough that most kids thought her mother was still around. But the lies and the losses took their toll. Jamaica grew up ashamed of her life, always afraid it would get worse.

It did. As a teenager, Jamaica was sent to one foster home and then another. The abuse at that second home has kept coming back and casting a shadow over her life now.

When Jamaica was twenty-two, alone with three kids, she got on a bus with nineteen dollars in her pocket, intent on leaving Chicago. "You think people want to live like that, all that killing and drugs everywhere? Ain't no way my kids was growin' up in that."

Sometimes she hung just on the edge. Once when I was visiting her home, she whispered to me, "I wish I was invisible. I wish I was homeless and just evaporated. But I can't do that 'cause of my kids. I gotta keep on for my kids." She would sink low, living out what had happened to her as a child, keeping on in the daily fight of poverty. Then she would pull herself together and focus on her children and on seeing that they did well. After a bad day she'd braid hair again, long hours making sure her daughters had their time with her and went out into the world neat and loved.

When the ghost wasn't in front of her, Jamaica was a joyous, open woman. She had a dry sense of humor and a strong religious faith that found the life in anything. She talked to you straight and quick, with a clear, deep love for her children. The first time I called Jamaica, she told me flat out the important things she wanted me to know: that she appreciated my working with Rebekka, and that her kids were supposed to do well and cause no problems in school. If they did, she wanted to hear about it.

Rebekka came from this home filled with deep love, deep worry, and deep depression. Always immaculately neat, she stood—a black child in a mostly white school—on the fringes, an icon of a child. There was a separateness that adults noticed in Rebekka right away. Standing or sitting right where she belonged, she held herself apart from everyone else there. She often had two fingers in her mouth; she would suck them as she observed what was around her. Her posture was straight. Deep adult eyes in a chiseled face, she was well behaved, kind, and removed. Everything about her bearing said, "Here is a boundary you cannot cross." She enjoyed school, but aside from the one friend she had decided to make, Rebekka stayed separate from people around her.

Halfway through first grade Rebekka could hardly read. Her demeanor—she had the self-possessed posture of a dancer—and the integrity of her isolation made you feel her strength. But it was also apparent what a burden it was for such a young child to carry around that strength.

Her purposiveness and the depth with which she could observe you made me certain she was capable of much more than she was doing in school. Rebekka was very willing to learn, but she wasn't understanding what she needed to. To teach Rebekka and find out what was going wrong in her learning, I had to both respect and reach through her distance. This was a child with an adult sense of boundaries. She needed that recognized.

Though Rebekka was at the bottom of her class halfway through first grade, she truly loved books. They were something she literally and symbolically held on to. Books had a sound and a look to them, and that seemed to matter more to her than the fact that when she read them they didn't make sense. A few words into a book, she would quickly make mistakes and veer away from meaning. Head close to the page, she would continue on intently, not stopping if something didn't make sense or even if she was inventing words. When I observed her before she started in Reading Recovery, she finished one book whose last sentence was *Then they all fell down,* confidently reading, "Then broke down with bowt." The meaning was gone, but there was a magic that held her.

From within her distance and isolation, Rebekka loved school and loved learning. She would pore over picture books, imagining their meaning as she looked closely at the pictures. She held her pencil carefully. She kept her supplies neat. She always wanted to do well.

Rebekka had picked up several isolated reading skills. She could identify all the letters in the alphabet except for two (she read *p* as *q* and *y* as *u*). She could correctly write nineteen words—the names of people in her family and the high-frequency words *a, I, to, dog, we, me, go, going, and, this, is, Mom, yes,* and *zoo* (*zoo* is a high-frequency word for first-graders).

Thus we had a firm base in letter identification and writing to start with. However, I suspected that Rebekka used memory as a main skill in her approach to reading. Memory helped her because she had developed good visual skills for whole words. But visual skills alone don't make a reader, or Rebekka wouldn't have been at the bottom of her class.

Although Rebekka had a sufficient written vocabulary, her writing showed a potential problem. In several words she wrote many letters—*c, t, s, p, d, N, e,* and *l*—as reversals. The fact that she wrote so many reversals could mean many things: that she wasn't looking closely at letters and so wasn't really taking in what they looked like; that it didn't yet matter to her that her letters look correct; or that she really wasn't seeing letters correctly. But the reversals were not Rebekka's only problem. They were a detail—a piece, but not the puzzle.

Rebekka's love of books meant that she was familiar with many concepts about them. She knew how to hold them and open them, what direction to read in, how to follow from line to line, and even how to point word by word on a page as I read. She knew what periods and question marks were, the relationship between capital and lowercase letters, the difference between words and letters, and the difference between the first and the last letter of a word. She could also hear sounds in words well, writing twenty-seven of the thirty-seven sounds in two sentences I dictated to her. Even so, Rebekka wasn't able to translate all these skills to fluent reading.

She could recognize letters, write words, hear sounds, and hold books with love, but she hadn't understood the importance of reading for meaning and of reading the words on the page—not ones she came up with in her head.

Like Rebekka, her skills were isolated. They had been built up and developed, but she hadn't learned how to bring them together. Just as Rebekka remained on the outside, observing, her skills remained outside each other, carefully honed, just as neat and precise as the cornrow girl with the classical dancer's face.

Aside from her difficulties with bringing her skills together, Rebekka faced two other major interferences in learning to read. First and most important, because Rebekka grew up poor with limited experience, she had a very small vocabulary. She didn't necessarily know the word she was trying to read. Visual analysis of concepts you don't understand is quite difficult. Rebekka was an observant, reflective child, and she felt this lack of words when she talked with you. Her response was often to make up the word she needed, and she did it quite well. One day, looking washed out and tight, walking slowly and deliberately on the way to our lesson, she explained to me, "My stomach twizzlin' today." Months later I asked Jamaica if "twizzle" was a word she used. She told me no and that Rebekka often made up words Jamaica had never heard before.

The other major block to Rebekka's reading was that she spoke in dialect, and the rules she knew for speaking Black English didn't always help her in predicting book language. Verbs repeatedly threw her off the whole time we worked together, because her verbs weren't conjugated like the ones in books. "I so scare the first day of school. I look up at nobody!" She couldn't draw on structure, or syntax, in learning to read, because syntax kept messing her up. Text either had extra words that she didn't expect or words that were longer than she expected, with different endings.

Taken as a whole, Rebekka had strong barriers to reading. She couldn't always use meaning in approaching words because of her limited vocabulary and because she hadn't yet completely understood that books are supposed to make sense, to tell a story. She couldn't always use language structure because book English isn't structured like Black English. And because she would glance off many words as she read them in text, and not check to make sure that they were right, she couldn't always use visual cues. Meaning, structure, and visual cues—she had problems with each element of reading. And then there was her distance, her security in standing removed from others.

But Rebekka loved books, so she was engrossed in them as soon as the first page was opened. With books Rebekka began to open up with me.

We started our first Roaming Around the Known session looking at Helen Oxenbury's *We're Going on a Bear Hunt*. Oxenbury's illustrations create a warm, exciting world where it's safe to imagine anything—including a bear chasing your family home. Our first day together, Rebekka recognized that the words to the story had a pattern to them, and after a few pages she tried reading along with me. On the second day she listened closely as I read the book to her again, and then she asked if she could read it. She read well, monitoring words and looking closely at each page. We spent twenty minutes that day on just *Bear Hunt* because she was so involved in the book. Twenty minutes is an awfully long time for a first-grader at the bottom of her class to spend engrossed in reading a book.

Bear Hunt became the framework for the first seven of our Roaming sessions, because Rebekka kept finding more and more in the book. "Why it say, '*We've* got to go through it' and not '*We* got to go through it'?" she asked, noticing that the text was written differently from the way she talked. She stared long and hard at the word *under,* confused by the *u* and the *n* because they were each other upside down and right next to each other. That similarity and contrast drew Rebekka's eye; to her the letters were the same, just in a different way.

I told her the two letters stood for different sounds. I named them and showed her how to make them. Children at the bottom of their first-grade class are usually eager and learning. But they're learning askew—thinking about how *n* and *u* mirror each other while the rest of the class is learning to monitor words. We need to hold on to their eagerness while we figure out what it is they are doing and move them to learning what they need to know.

I picked Rebekka up from her classroom each day for lessons, and in our walks she began to talk more. Rebekka's form of trust came through questions. Because Rebekka and I were alone and no other child could interrupt us, I could answer all her questions and show I respected them. She was allowed her own pace; her distance was accepted. And comfortable with that acceptance, Rebekka started opening up.

Once she began to speak regularly with me, I became a way for her to voice her constant wonder. She asked me about the world so she could know more about it. In answering her questions, I made everything more real—her recognized self, the world, and me, her own individual teacher, someone that she knew really saw her.

"Do people shrink? You know, when you washin' 'em? Can you wash a kid? Can you put 'em in a dryer?"

"That'd be pretty dangerous."

"How 'bout a washin' machine?"

"You want to get washed in a washing machine?"

"Uh-uh!"

Had she been in a middle-class home with parents who answered most of her questions about life, Rebekka would have built up quite a vocabulary. But Rebekka's mother, Jamaica, had to focus on more pressing problems—making sure she and her four kids weren't living on the street, making sure they had food, making sure she got through each day. Poverty wears you down, and it teaches you few words to know life through. Poverty was really Rebekka's major barrier to learning.

Each day in Roaming, Rebekka would return to what she needed in *Bear Hunt.* She asked me again about *through,* and this time it was clear she didn't understand the meaning of the word. I took her through the doorway, I took her through the hall, and I talked about how we were moving *through* them. But it took several days for Rebekka to understand this spatial concept.

One of the ways in which Rebekka learned was by talking about whatever she was doing as she did it. Her monologues were often a great check for me on how well she understood what I had taught. A few days after we had had our first walk through the doorway and through the hall, she was reading *Bear Hunt* to me and then looked up from the page.

"You know how I read this book? I be memborizing when I read it with you."

She read a few more lines and stopped again.

"Why do the words 'pear and 'pear again?"

I told her about repetition and how it helped make the book so scary and fun. She read on.

"What he mean *through?*"

We talked again about this spatial concept, how it means moving from one side to another of something. I wasn't sure if she was confused by the homonym *threw* or by the difference between what the word looked like and her pronunciation of it in Black English, "frew." I showed her in the book the family going through a river, through grass, through a snowstorm, through a forest. She listened quietly and seriously, looking at me the whole time, and then read on until she got almost to the end of the book. I think each time she read *through* it made a little more sense to her. Almost at the end of the book, too excited to keep reading without discussing it, she turned to me, saying, "I can't wait 'til I get to the bear part!" and raised her hands in the air like she was scoring a touchdown. Rebekka now knew a book well enough to predict its meaning, to expect confidently what was coming. A week into Roaming, she was reading a long book in a different way than she ever had been able to before.

Rebekka's obvious proficiency with *Bear Hunt* had made her sure enough so that if she reached a problem word she would say excitedly, "Don't tell me! Don't tell me!" and try to figure the word out. She both recognized when a word was hard and worked on it. But as she grew more confident and involved, I saw more and more how limited her vocabulary was.

One day she was working on the book she was writing, "My Mommy and Me." Rebekka talked to me as she drew her mother and herself in the living room but then stopped because she didn't know a word.

"That window broke. Lots o' windows. We cold. When people don't have no—what you call that thing you put up?"

"Curtain?"

"Yeah. When people don't have no curtain, why they put up blankets?"

I talked to Rebekka about how her mother probably did that to keep the room warmer. That was all Rebekka needed to know. She kept on drawing and concentrated on the furniture in her picture. I started worrying about how her family was getting through the winter.

Rebekka was poor and had a limited number of words to think with. But she gave herself to learning with intensity. In Roaming, Rebekka started to break down her separateness and to trust me. She wanted to take in as much as she could about the world around her, about books, about whatever came into her head, and she risked letting me know that part of her. I could answer questions, and for the first time Rebekka had an adult's undivided attention in both explaining the world and recognizing her. Her willingness to ask questions gave her a chance to become a good student. In a few years Rebekka, unaided, would have been used to being at the bottom of her class and would have been wary of opening up like this. Now was the time to catch her, to help her achieve in school.

In our semester together I became a dictionary for Rebekka, and on the way to class or in the middle of writing, she would pump me for more and more words. "What you call those roses but they get real big?" I figured out she meant tulips. "What you call these things on my sweater?" I told her sparkles. Life was so big, Rebekka wanted more names for it. Her stories and conversations with me got more form and detail as Rebekka's vocabulary grew. If you don't have words to think with, it stunts how you can think.

In our two weeks in Roaming, Rebekka went back day after day to a difficult, long book—one with strange words like *gloomy, goggly,* and *through* that were far beyond her vocabulary—and learned to read it fluently. My original plan had been to read *Bear Hunt* to Rebekka and let her just enjoy the story and pictures. But Rebekka was so clearly hooked by the book that it took over what we did; it became truly her book as she asked and learned, asked and learned. She looked so closely at words in the book that she learned what it feels like to monitor when reading. (Not that she did monitor consistently even now, but she had the experience to draw on.) She glanced at pictures to remember words. She corrected mistakes because she noticed them.

Because of Roaming, Rebekka could now look at books much more carefully than she had been able to two weeks before. When lessons started, we moved through four levels of books in ten lessons—quick, solid progress—because her love of story, combined now with looking at words, helped her read much more fluently.

Rebekka was eager for every book we read, and now that she had opened up with me, she wasn't an outsider. As a practiced observer, Rebekka had recognized that I saw and accepted her. That complicity of recognition became our link, and now Rebekka wasn't reluctant to talk.

Rebekka often told me all about books before we started— a clear sign of reading for meaning. "Oh, this one one of my favorites. The dog gonna try to help here, but he gonna make a mess instead!"

But then, once she was reading, she became much less aware of me. That separateness would return as she moved forward toward the book, eyes intent on the page. They would glide back and forth between the pictures and the words, as she really thought about what she read and enjoyed the illustrations. As Rebekka withdrew from me into reading, the intensity of her connection to the book showed the strength she had always gotten from her separateness at school. I was not there. It was Rebekka and the book. There was an integrity to her isolation, a strong world that she created for herself.

Rebekka's profound connection with books wasn't from confidence in reading; it was at a deeper level, in the pleasure of the text. The child who had made herself separate—and from that distance observed what was around her—was now closely observing what books were.

But as we moved into harder books, it quickly became clear that her love of books wasn't enough. Rebekka didn't have the strategies to deal with mistakes when she read. She would glide over them, ignoring her errors. Or, if she recognized an error, she would iterate the wrong word without attempting something new, for example, "she-she-she-she" for *her.* I taught her the skills of checking the first letter of a word and checking to see if a word made sense, and she used these skills to gain more independence in reading.

Children who aren't learning to read well often don't realize that the reason we read is to understand things, to know them. They focus (or don't focus) on the letters in the text and stay at that level. As I kept asking Rebekka "Does that make sense?" "Does that look like what you just said?" books opened up to her in a larger way. Rebekka was learning to go beyond observation to comparison. She was on the edge of moving from the essential question of her distanced observation, "What is this?" to a more integrated question, "What does it mean?" In putting together reading, she was journeying from being to signification, from isolation to connection.

But as books opened up to her at a larger level, Rebekka continued to write letters and words as reversals. For example, she would first try "if" and then "ti" for *it* (the shapes of *f* and D'Nealian *t* are quite similar). She wrote "ym" for *my,* and "doG" was *dog.* She randomly wrote *l, t,* and *s* backward.

In one of our first lessons, after Rebekka wrote a word backward, I talked with her about directionality and drew an arrow pointing to the right, to emphasize that we always read words and sentences from left to right.

"How'd you make that thing?" she asked immediately. Another sign of Rebekka's limited vocabulary—she didn't know the word *arrow.*

"What?"

"That thing there." She pointed to the arrow. "Show me how to make that." I told her the name, *arrow,* and drew an arrow slowly, describing the line and the v on its side that make it up as I did so. Rebekka tried to copy it and drew an arrow with the v facing the opposite direction. Though I tried to describe and model what I was doing in a few different ways, Rebekka could only come up with the v backward. We dropped this exercise so that I could get her back to writing and reading, but I was starting to become concerned with how often Rebekka wrote letters and words backward. That she couldn't copy a fairly simple shape, even with guidance, made me feel I needed to get another opinion and more information on how she was doing in class.

Rebekka's classroom teacher was one of the first in Madison to move away from basal teaching to a whole language classroom. Children in her class write daily, and she keeps careful track of their progress. She saw Rebekka having the same problems I saw but tied them to her limited experience with books and writing before she had come to school. Once Rebekka was writing more and reading more, her teacher thought she would probably get the reversal problem under control.

Talking with another teacher, rather than trying to figure Rebekka out on my own, helped me keep my focus in teaching reading to her. The obvious signals that kids send out about the problems they are having in reading and writing can sometimes get our attention more easily than the deeper blocks they are having in learning to read fluently.

Fluent readers read letters in words as parts of a whole sign and whole representation.* Rebekka had not yet learned to see small two-dimensional signs (i.e., letters) closely enough to have fully learned their shapes or to remember how to write them. In learning to see words, most children need to go through a period of consciously looking closely and associating symbol with sound and meaning. Rebekka's frequent reversals were an indication that she needed more time in this period of acquiring firm knowledge about the form and direction of letters and words. But they did not mean that she should be kept from learning to read harder and harder books because, more important, Rebekka needed to continue to learn to read text for meaning. She was just beginning to understand the power of thinking about what she read.

For Rebekka, fluency in the written form of letters was going to come with increased fluency in reading. Her reversals were a detail, and if I had taught primarily to her details, Rebekka would have failed.

Some young children respond particularly strongly to poetry, and Rebekka was one of these children. One of my favorite books to teach in Reading Recovery is *The Wind* by Barbara Hill. It is a poem that slowly builds through repetition, page after page recording more and more of what the wind blows.

---

* One aspect of reading that continues to amaze me is that when we do it well we can forget we're reading. If we were constantly aware of seeing each word on the page, we would not be able to fluidly construct meaning as we read. At a certain fluent level of reading, words become invisible because they *become* their meaning.

The illustrations by Rosemary Turner set it apart. They have vivid colors and strong forms, and they look more formal than many children's book illustrations. To the children who notice the relationship between the sound of the words and the pictures, this is *literature* in their hands.

The book is twelve pages long with ten lines of text, and on the last page the poem that has built over the preceding pages is repeated in stanza form, now without pictures to help the child check meaning:

> The wind
> The wind blows...
>
> The wind blows the trees
> and the leaves
> and the birds
> and the sea.
>
> The wind blows the dirt
> and the shirt
> and my skirt
> and ME!

Rebekka, an isolated child mesmerized by words, was overtaken by this book. She felt a sense of power, reading its difficult final page with no clear picture cues. When she read, you heard the cadence and the majesty of the repetitions. Face serious and intent, you saw her feel the solemnity that this was literary language, these words were spoken for a different reason. Nicholas worked hard with me because he knew it was his chance not to fail; Nkauj Hli worked hard because it helped her make sense of school. Rebekka worked hard because she loved books. They were hers and she was theirs as she leaned into them, finding out now what they meant.

Rebekka took *The Wind* home to read that weekend and for more several nights. The day after she first took it home, I heard on our walk to my room about everyone she had read it to. "I read it to my daddy, and he said I sure can read. I read it to my mom, too. And I sat by myself with it and read it to me."

Rebekka was a different reader after *The Wind,* because she knew now that she could read poetry and that she could read words on a page with no pictures to help. *The Wind* was a benchmark for her because she felt that she had excelled in school, that she had learned here in a deeper way. She still was behind her classmates (ironically, now that she was doing better she was more aware of this), but she knew now what it felt like to focus in on and do well at exactly what the teacher had asked her to learn.

After *The Wind,* Rebekka approached difficult words differently, making repeated attempts on them and wanting them to make sense. For *in,* finger firmly on the word, she tried, "Over-under-on-in-over-on-in-over-on-over-in-over-in-as-behind-behind-behind." She didn't have fully enough developed reading strategies to notice when she did read the word correctly, so she continued making other attempts. But this was a withdrawn girl from the bottom of her class who had just persevered in making seventeen attempts to read one word correctly, who had over and over tried to read a word as the part of speech it was, a preposition. Starting to more surely draw on language structure in reading, she was gaining amazing independence, focus, and the desire to make things right.

The more I have taught, the more I have understood the crucial importance of children learning to attend to print, to monitor, and to cross-check. As the first becomes established, it transforms into the next. As children become accustomed to seeing and saying words in the right order and reading only the number of words that are on the page—the essence of attending to print—they begin to look more closely at each word. They become aware of reading whole words that they know, of seeing the first letter of words they are predicting. In doing so, they are monitoring.

But looking at and thinking about the sounds of letters does not take you all the way to meaning. That strategy stops at the graphic representation of a word. So from the beginning children in Reading Recovery are taught to ask themselves questions about meaning and structure: "Does that make sense?" "Does it look right?" As they ask themselves questions based on the three linguistic elements of written language—meaning, structure, and visual cues—they begin to learn to cross-check. Cross-checking brings the reader and the text much closer because the child has to think about the meaning of the words she sees.

For Rebekka, considering larger questions of meaning as she read and stopping to check the text to see if she was right was becoming a new way of reading and of being in school. Before, she had observed and imagined, and drawn into herself in doing so. Now, questioning and checking, she was learning to establish a different connection with what she read. She could not pull back from the books and still know if she had read them right. Cross-checking is bringing at least two elements of language together. For Rebekka, it also meant bringing herself and the book closer together.

After Rebekka started drawing on cross-checking in reading, both her relationship with books and her questions to me changed. The questions she had asked me until now had been about vocabulary she was curious about in her daily life but didn't know. Now her questions were turning more to text. She noticed the apostrophe in *what's* and asked, "How they put a 'postrophe be front of the *s?*" Rebekka so loved words that she held them in her mind. Because *an* was not a word in Rebekka's syntax, she heard and memorized *apostrophe* as "a postrophe."

As an interior, reflective child who observed more than participated, Rebekka was still very fanciful and imaginative in her thinking. I think that was part of her love of books. Books were not just there—she imagined them having been written and made by someone. Rebekka thought about books and thought about their origins. I could imagine her seeing someone putting that "postrophe" into *what's* to make it a strange-looking word. We talked about contractions and what they mean, but I think Rebekka was still most impressed by the look, by the form of the word, by those people putting a mark in front of the *s*. She was at a much deeper level than understanding grammatical representation. She was imagining connection and purpose. A girl who had been connected to almost no one now imagined a connection to a book's author.

Rebekka's increased confidence and the closer monitoring she had started to pick up in Roaming had been enough to help her breeze through the first eight levels of books. But now she was reading books with longer words, harder words, and more involved story lines. In learning more skills of word analysis, she started to back away from cross-checking and reverted to the kind of reading she had been doing before Reading Recovery, just at a higher level.

She was beginning to look more closely at words, to start to see across them. But as she focused on looking at the word, she forgot to check if it made any sense or sounded right. In lesson sixteen she read "all-on-yed" for *allowed* and "abring-aber-abrought" for *absolute.*

However, these errors showed that Rebekka was now looking at more than the first and last letter of a word. She was making tentative steps toward scanning words. In lesson eighteen one of her errors showed she was starting to use chunks of words or syllables when she read, to break down long words, reading "behind-be. . . k-be. . . s-behind-became" for *because.*

Rebekka knew now that she was making errors, but again, in harder text, she didn't know what to do about them. When she was engrossed in a book, she was curled over it, her perfect, cornrow-framed face silhouetted, still, as her index finger pointed under every word, a moving line connecting Rebekka and the book.

But when she stumbled with errors, Rebekka's hand would slip into her lap and rest there. Her silhouette was just as still, but now Rebekka was an eighty-year-old woman who has seen too much of life and accepted failure. Her eyes had given up, and her skin looked gray. It took all her energy and grace to just sit, remain.

"Rebekka," I said quietly. "Do you have a voice in your head telling you this is too hard, and you can't do it?"

She turned and looked at me, taken aback. "How you know?"

"Is it saying, 'Rebekka Booker, you can't read this 'cause you're not smart enough'?"

She nodded, stunned that I could hear her thoughts.

"Did you know that everybody has voices like that in their head at times?" She shook her head silently no. "And you don't have to listen to that voice. What's it know? Nothing. I'm your teacher, and I know you're smart."

Rebekka wasn't letting go of a word I said.

"I want you to have another voice in your head saying, 'Rebekka Booker, you are one smart cookie.'" She nodded. "Say it. 'Rebekka Booker, you are one smart cookie.'"

"Rebekka Booker, you are one smart cookie," she whispered.

"Say it again, because this is an important thing to know."

"Rebekka Booker, you are one smart cookie."

"Now next time that voice says you can't do something in school, you just say, 'Get out of here. I'm one smart cookie,' and you'll see. It'll go away. Not right away all the time. But you'll make it go away."

Rebekka nodded again. This matter was too serious for her to want to talk about. She needed to take it in on her own.

We went back to the lesson and focused on cross-checking, being aware of a word in more than one way, so that she could get herself out of her confusions when she knew a word was wrong. "Does it look right?" "Does it make sense?" "Can we say it that way?" were all questions for Rebekka to ask herself when she came to a hard word. You could also see she was trying out thinking she might be smart.

As Rebekka was getting her book to take home at the end of the lesson that day, I told her, "Now I want you to say it to yourself all the way back to class. 'Rebekka Booker, you are one smart cookie. Rebekka Booker, you are one smart cookie.'" She smiled up at me, her fairy godmother who had just turned her into a princess. "And I want you to say it to yourself in class, too. This is a powerful voice to use." Rebekka nodded, gave me a hug, and looked at me with a tight smile that knew we were thinking the same thing at the same time. I watched her as she walked through the gym, on her way back to class, book swinging in its plastic bag next to her, and I knew she was saying, "Rebekka Booker, you are one smart cookie. Rebekka Booker, you are one smart cookie."

Rebekka was now increasing the circle of people she trusted. I introduced her to teachers on the playground, my arm around her, telling them what a great kid she was. Rebekka didn't start out removed with them; she took them on faith. She would tilt her head and ask them a question, or just stand, basking in being seen. It was spring, and there was an ease in being outside again in warmer weather. Sometimes she would simply stand with me at recess and smile, enjoying sharing the day.

Always, wanting to know more about the world, wanting more names for it, she asked questions. At Easter her family was going down to Illinois to visit her father. Rebekka regaled me with the details of all the things they would be doing there—getting some new clothes, going on an Easter egg hunt—and she finished with the most important.

"I'm gonna meet my daddy's daddy."

"That's your grandpa, Rebekka."

"My grandpa?"

"Yeah. Your daddy's daddy is your grandpa."

"He my grandpa?"

Rebekka walked along silently for a moment, taking this in. Then, wanting more: "Do every grandpa have a grandpa woman?" I told her no, not always, and that "grandpa women" are usually called *grandmas.*

Rebekka nodded and pondered this. She was taking it in and didn't need me to be a part of her musings. I had learned that Rebekka often withdrew to think after an important question was answered. We walked in silence the rest of the way to my room.

We were reading more difficult books with more varied and irregular verbs, and Rebekka's natural syntax in Black English at times still kept her from reading the words that were in the book. In her twentieth lesson Rebekka made eleven errors, eight of which were tense based. For example, she read "pick" for *picked,* "wash" for *washed,* "get" for *got.* I told her that she had to learn this different way of talking to read well, that it was school talk and book talk, and asked her in carefully chosen words if she had noticed the difference between the way her classroom teacher and I talked and how she talked.

Rebekka looked at me in disbelief, surprised this was even a question to ask. "Yeah! You white."

I laughed out loud at how blunt she was in answering and then continued. Rebekka said what was in her mind, not knowing enough yet to be awkward.

I told her most books were written the way her teacher and I talked. Not all of them. But to read books well now, she had to attend to how books sound. I told her to hold on to how she talked and be proud of it. She used words like a writer. But she had to learn book English, too.

This was Rebekka in a foreign country. Now that she knew so much more about reading and had gotten so much closer to books' words, she was having to figure out how to get over the gulf of reading books that again and again sounded like the white kids she knew but not like her. It meant I had to reinforce careful monitoring, because when Rebekka made structural errors, they did sound right to her and they did make sense to her. They just weren't what was in the book.

To help her learn how to read new words, I kept teaching her to both look at words and use meaning in thinking about them. I could see this become a skill she drew on more and more, because Rebekka was more consistently using cross-checking. In the book for lesson twenty-two, *The Biggest Cake in the World* by Joy Cowley, the cake is so big that Mrs. Delicious has to use a chainsaw to cut it. Rebekka read, "Cut— What you call that saw?—motorcycle-cut" for *chainsaw.*

Her reading attempts now used real words and generally made sense. This was a big shift from reading "all-on-yed" as a word just six lessons before. Rebekka was applying meaning as she was looking at words. I think she said "motorcycle" for *chainsaw* because she was thinking of the similar noise they make and trying to get to the *chain* part of the word with that analogy.

She would comment as she worked things out, like when she read *Marmalade's Nap* by Cindy Wheeler, the story of a cat trying to find somewhere quiet to sleep on a farm: "Perk-ch-puleep-pee...Do birds really say that? Pull-baby-buh...Wait, it, it was, what was it?...baby."

These were the same kind of monologues that Rebekka had had in Roaming with "Why do the words 'pear and 'pear again?" and "What he mean *through?*" But now, more important, they were cross-checking questions directed at meaning (she could read the word *peep,* but it sounded like nonsense to her and nonsense wasn't good enough now), and she was asking herself the questions first, not turning to me.

Now when something didn't make sense, Rebekka would stop. Continuing that day with *Marmalade's Nap,* she read, "Eeleeven-noisy-noisy-ellowed-even" for *everywhere.* Rebekka sat, stuck, so I told her the word. She looked up at me quickly. By telling her the word, I had become involved in her reading process, and she asked me, confused, "What he mean 'every-where?'" Two months earlier, it wouldn't have mattered to her that what she read make sense. Books then were words and pictures. Now they were meaning. They were also clearly written *by* someone, which I don't think was as important to her a few months before when books were a haven, pictures to get lost in, but not an extended story.

Most young kids, unless they are reading a favorite author, don't really think of a school book as being written by some-one. For Rebekka it wasn't just that the book had meaning, it was that "he mean" something in writing it. She was aware of the book as a symbolic act, a conscious expression of story-telling. In thinking about the book, she felt a connection to the real person who wrote it. This connection ran parallel to Rebekka's burgeoning connection to specific people at school. Just as Rebekka was moving away from her isolation at school and starting to become connected to people, her connection to books was changing, too. They weren't just books, they weren't just fantasy. They were books and fantasy written by real people. Rebekka could open up more to us because she was learning how to open up to and understand books.

Her writing was making huge leaps, too. She wrote the entire word *sister* on her own. When I asked her how she did it, she replied, "I be member it in my head." I think Rebekka's fantastic control over writing was in fact because she did "be member" things; when she looked at words, they became hers.

Poor kids can't help but filter school through their difference, and part of their learning is learning they have less materially than other kids. This can grind them down until *they* are less. What my own children can take for granted—warmth, food, knowing where they'll be living next month—makes it easier for them to learn and to do well in school. Many children who live in poverty bring the lack of these securities with them to school every day.

Rebekka knew her difference, knew she went to the free breakfast program in the morning and ate a free lunch at noon. One day Rebekka brought her lunch to school, something the kids who get free lunch rarely do. As soon as I picked her up for our lesson, she was talking to me about it and wanted to make sure I saw this amazing meal. We went to her locker so that Rebekka could get her book, and she pulled out, instead, her lunch.

"Everybody think this is the first time I'm having cold lunch. You wanna see it? My mama make it." She slowed down now, savoring the display. Each part of the lunch came out of the bag slowly, and Rebekka's words were drawn out to match the demonstration, her intonation rising with each pause. "I got a bag of chips...two submarines...a piece of cake—but it's bent here—and a juice in a bag, so it don't spill all over everything."

This lunch made Rebekka feel like one of the kids who get to choose whether or not to eat school lunch. It was a luxury day, and after we got the lunch back in the bag, back in the locker, locker door closed, book in hand, Rebekka told me about her lunch all over again as we walked to my room. I didn't know it, but this lunch meant Jamaica was cleaning out the refrigerator and leaving early for spring break to go take care of a relative who was ill. It was the last I saw of Rebekka for almost three weeks.

Her first day back from Illinois, Rebekka told me right away, "I didn't see you 'bout any days. I kep' on saying, 'Ms. O'Leary, Ms. O'Leary,' but nobody didn't hear me."

She went on then, telling me about her trip. She never met her grandpa, but her daddy did take her to an Easter egg hunt, and Rebekka and her brothers and sisters had found an amazing number of different-colored eggs. In the middle of telling me about the hunt, Rebekka interrupted herself and said, "What color should Easter be on?" I asked her what she meant, and it just seemed to her that the day Easter should have a color. Purple seemed good to me. It did to her, too.

Rebekka's writing vocabulary was growing so quickly that we no longer took words to fluency at the beginning of the lesson. In lesson twenty-nine she wrote *with* correctly, remembering what it looked like in the book, even though she pronounced the word as "wif." The sentence she wrote that day about *TJ's Tree* by Marcia Vaughn was "<u>They</u> <u>filled</u> <u>the</u> <u>hole</u> <u>with</u> <u>soil</u>." This was a first-grader hearing vowel sounds and using silent *e* and the *-ed* ending correctly. Rebekka had started Reading Recovery with isolated skills that she couldn't bring together to read and write fluently. She now was transferring close monitoring of print in books to more advanced writing. And her reversals, with attention but not primary emphasis on them, had almost disappeared.

Rebekka's rapid progress was now becoming her main problem. She could see herself getting more and more control over writing; she could hear herself reading fluently. With this sense of ownership of words and books, she now wanted to rush at them, to intensify the connection. In chasing the books, she read fluently but not closely. Her errors teetered around the words on the page but showed she wasn't carefully monitoring. For example, she read "has" for *had,* "sock" for *socks,* "laugh" for *laughed.* We talked about slowing down, about making sure she looked at every word as she read. All of her tense and plural errors were meaningful, but I wanted more for Rebekka than approximations. If she could focus on and discipline her reading, she could learn to read anything.

When I would coach her to slow down, Rebekka would approach the book more closely, physically moving in to it, a triangle with the table, left hand on chin, right index finger pointing from word to word as she connected to every word she saw. But without my reminders Rebekka would speed up again, intent on the chase of reading. My teaching points over and over were simply, "Slow down," and "Look at what you read."

Rebekka could memorize words, but she couldn't always expect them. Reading standard English through a dialect, reading words whose meaning she didn't know because of her small vocabulary, sometimes overwhelmed her. As she sat staring at her book, her confidence would drain away, and though she was already silent, she would become quieter. Her dignified child's brown face would turn gray, and she would become again that resigned old woman.

The grayness was always startling, because Rebekka was a beautiful, intense girl. But her confusion had transformed her because books were her connection to school, to life outside her home. In learning to find meaning in and trust books, she was learning to open up more to people around her. If she failed to make sense out of reading, she failed to keep her connection to school. When she knew she didn't understand what she read, she had already lived life, and it had been too hard.

On those days, if Rebekka made an error, she would sit for a few beats, aware of it, and then read on. She didn't try to correct mistakes, she didn't try to use the skills she had acquired. She sat resigned, one hand in her lap and one hand—only because I had insisted on it—moving slowly beneath words she felt were larger than her. On those days, Rebekka would listen sadly to all I said but believe little of it. The voice was back in her head telling her she couldn't do it.

Rebekka stood out from other children to me because books were such a tangible, crucial symbol to her. She loved holding them and reading them, unlocking what they meant. To come up against defeat in something that mattered so much pulled her back into her withdrawal and isolation. And now there was a consciousness of failure that hadn't been there before. Books were more than books to her. They were her dignity, her most sure connection to the world.

Most children have only a few years in which to gain confidence in reading. If they don't think they read well by second grade, odds are they never will think they read well. Older children and adults who struggle in reading have learned too well that they don't know. Even if they read something simple well, they don't feel confident, because they know it is simple and they should read better.

Illiterate children and adults who try to get better at reading have unfortunately learned monitoring not as "Does what I read make sense?" but as "Am I making sense?" They monitor themselves more than the page and see failure. Older children and adults can learn to read, but in order to do so, they have to fight off their own sense of failure. First-graders see themselves failing, too, but they are not so used to it. It is easier to teach a six-year-old to be confident than a twelve-year-old who has had years at the bottom of the class. That is why it is so important to catch children early, to find them in their first moments of self-defeat. Rebekka's sense of defeat in reading was especially disturbing because books had been her means of opening up in school.

But Rebekka's deep feelings of failure also held real promise. When I first started working with her, she loved school but sat quietly unaware of how poorly she was doing. She had been slowly learning, but she hadn't been learning at anywhere near the pace she was capable of. Now in Reading Recovery, she knew she knew much more. She was pushing herself, and she didn't get a break, because I was always taking her, as soon as she was ready, to the next step. Now she knew her failure when she saw it, and now she didn't want to fail. We were on a precipice.

I wanted Rebekka to be aware of the times when she felt capable so that she wouldn't start to see herself primarily as a failure. We still worked on fighting off that voice telling her she couldn't do things. Now, too, when Rebekka was reading fluently, I started asking her to recognize it, to know success.

"Do you feel what it's like to look closely at your words?"

"Uh-huh," she said slowly, trying not to smile.

"What's it like?"

Rebekka quickly put her face in her hands to hide it, embarrassed that we were talking about her doing well.

"Say it in your own words, Rebekka."

She peeked up at me through one hand and fixed her eyes on me. Then, sure I would give her the answer, she said excitedly, "I give up!" She could feel what I was talking about but didn't have the words for it. But she was ready for me to tell her just exactly how she felt, because this felt so good she wanted to know what it was.

I told her I wouldn't be telling her the answer. Instead, I wanted her to watch for this feeling again when she read well and tell me in her own words what it was. She didn't have to tell me right away; just watch, and she'd know. She looked at me solemnly, still behind her hands, and nodded.

We kept working together, trying to get Rebekka to pay closer attention to words as she read and to recognize when she did well. The past tense remained hard for her because she usually didn't use past tense inflections when she spoke. She was now just starting to look for the past tense of verbs when she read, but she immediately ran into the problem of the many common irregular verbs. One day she read "rise-roe-rie-ra-rens-shine-rees" for *rose,* "blowed" for *blew,* "fall-falled" for *fell,* and "drink" for *drank.* A child who spoke standard English would not have had this roadblock to fluent reading.

When Nkauj Hli or other ESL students learn to speak and read English, that's just what they have to do to make any sense of school. English is clearly not their native language—it has different rules, different vocabulary, and different structure.

But Black English is a variant of standard American English. It is close enough that African Americans who speak it can obviously understand standard English. The two share similar core vocabulary and many grammatical rules. Yet if African American children who speak Black English start learning to use standard English—which sounds awfully white to them—that can mean a sliding over into being someone else. Switching from one dialect to another calls into question—if only as a funny feeling in your stomach—your race, your class, your connection to family and friends, your sense of who you are.

Jamaica's children had an injunction "Do well in school." I talked to Jamaica several times on the phone, I met her twice during the school year, and we enjoyed working together to make sure Rebekka did well. Jamaica made sure Rebekka read those books at home every night and then got the books back in her backpack. But even with all this support, and the feeling that home and school worked together, learning to think about language differently was a real struggle. Kids who come to reading through dialect have to work harder just to keep up.

And Rebekka was working harder. She was exhilarated by how well she was doing, by the way books were becoming more and more her own. And that remained her problem. When she felt really confident, she read fast and made mistakes that were meaningful because they sounded like she talked. When she lost her confidence, she slowed down, but she also no longer thought she could read. Books were bigger than Rebekka then, and the errors she made no longer brought meaning to the text.

In our last lessons I was constantly balancing confidence and fluency as I taught. To keep Rebekka reading fluently, I had to keep her confidence up, keep her aware of success. At the same time, to teach her to read fluently without me, I had to bring her attention to the parts of words she kept missing and teach her to read for detail, even though I knew she understood the whole. For example, I focused on verb endings because Rebekka's native sense of how verbs sounded kept overriding what she actually saw in print.

But she *was* reading for meaning, and if something didn't make sense, she would stop. In *Pancakes for Supper* by Cheryl Semple and Judy Tuer, lesson thirty-seven, for the sentence "Stir it all together," Rebekka persevered on *together,* reading "to-to... great... the-to... great" and then just sat, puzzled by the word. When I told her it was *together,* she looked at me still puzzled, and said, "They stirrin' it all together?" To Rebekka that meant that both girls were stirring, not that one was mixing all the ingredients. She had stopped in her reading because it now mattered to her that what she read make sense.

Rebekka continued to learn easily to write more and more words: *milk* and *please,* which meant she had recognized and taken in some of the meaning of the double-vowel rule.

In her fortieth lesson, excited about the clothes she had received over the weekend as a present, Rebekka wrote, "I went to JC Penney's for clothes." As I wrote the *t-h-e* in *clothes* for Rebekka, I quickly explained that the word *clothes* came from *cloth* and that hundreds of years ago people used to say *cloth-es.* (I've always thought that knowing that most spelling does make sense helps kids to understand it better, to believe the magic in words.)

But Rebekka's mind was racing backward, imagining hundreds and hundreds of years as she listened to me. She looked at me intensely, much further in thought than *cloth-es* and *clothes.* She whispered seriously, "When we wasn't born, who was there? Was the animals still alive?"

Those questions were the essence of Rebekka: creative, imaginative, eager to learn more and more. Before she learned to read, she didn't know how, or wasn't sure enough, to show this side of herself easily in school. Because her speech was so far from school English, it was much harder for her to learn to read than for kids who grew up speaking standard English. But it also was beautifully poetic in its dissonance with standard grammar and concepts of time: "Was the animals still alive?" Rebekka hadn't been sitting tuned out and incapable at the bottom of her class; she had been pondering large questions that took her imagination far away: "Who was there?"

Reading Recovery gave Rebekka the chance to learn the practice of focusing on the point at hand. In the classroom Rebekka would have been lost for several minutes in her questions. Here I could acknowledge her questions and then quickly pull her back to learning what I wanted to teach, giving her the experience of paying attention in class. In learning to read, she was learning to learn.

In that same lesson I introduced Margaret Wise Brown's *Goodnight Moon* to Rebekka for the next day's Running Record. It is a lovely, magical nighttime book for small children in which a young rabbit slowly goes to sleep by saying goodnight to everything around him. It is quiet, rhythmic, and enchanting; the repetition of the goodnights draws you in and slows you down. First-graders love this book, love being the real reader who can recite its subtly changing words. Rebekka, beyond the sounds, was drawn into the book's world. She sat closer to it and focused intently on the words.

Two lessons later, when she was reading the first part of *Goodnight Moon* for fluency, she read "Goodnight great green room" for "In the great green room" but then went back and corrected her reading. She had internalized the skills of cross-checking visual cues against meaning, visual cues against structure. She knew that what she had said didn't look like what was in the book.

When I asked her how she had fixed her mistake, she said, "I didn't see 'in.' I messed up on this part until I went back and started again."

"How did you know to go back?"

"It didn't lookted right."

Like Nkauj Hli, Rebekka had become conscious of using the past tense but hadn't yet figured out what to do with the two pronunciations we use for *-ed*, "t" and "ed." She knew, though, that she had to monitor her reading, and this monitoring was surfacing in her spoken English, too.

The rabbit at various points in the book says, "Goodnight moon" and "Goodnight room." When she continued with the last half of the book that day for her Running Record, Rebekka read *room* for *moon* and then corrected it. After she had finished reading, I went back to her correction and asked her again how she had known to do it. She pointed closely to *moon* and said, "It don't start the same. First they switch the *m* and the *n*, and then they put the *r* at the front. But it's *room* and *moon*."

For Rebekka, this was a real, almost alive book, created by real people. She could see those people moving those letters around, creating different words. This close reading of and thinking about text showed how far Rebekka had come. Less than four months before, she had been reading "Then broke down with bowt" for *Then they all fell down* as meaningful and visually correct.

When our lesson was over that day, and Rebekka was carefully putting *Goodnight Moon* in her bag to take home to read, she stopped and asked me quietly, "Is this story real?"

That magical sense of fantasy and reality that six-year-olds carry around in them, and that adults often fail to see, had again surfaced. The young rabbit, wearing pajamas, is going to bed in a spacious 1940s children's bedroom. A quiet old lady rabbit, also in clothes, sits in the room for part of the book, rocking and knitting, whispering "Hush," and then eventually leaves. To an adult, *Goodnight Moon* is a beautiful book but far from real. To a child like Rebekka, the imaginary is real, and entering this real world makes her love of reading that much stronger. Rebekka's delight and belief in books repeatedly reminded me why a child would want to learn to read. Books were a context for Rebekka's imagination; they made her world larger and more accessible.

When Rebekka and I had started together, she loved books but couldn't read a page with two lines of print. By the end of the year she was reading *Frog and Toad Are Friends* by Arnold Lobel and *Henry and Mudge* by Cynthia Rylant at home. They were hard for her, but she kept at them until she could read them fluently. She would bring them to me and ask if we could practice them at the beginning of the lesson, so that she could get help on the hard parts.

Learning to read changed what Rebekka's life could be. She became more sure of herself, she asked questions more easily, and she opened up more to people around her. I was a part of that happening, but Rebekka's deep desire to learn and know was the most important part.

When Jamaica and I talked at the end of school, she talked to me straight, the way Jamaica always could, about Rebekka's and my relationship as student and teacher.

"She chose you," Jamaica told me firmly. "Rebekka don't warm up to most people and don't trust 'em. But she chose you, and I want you to know that."

Rebekka chose me because I recognized her, because she realized I was trying to see who she was and to teach what she needed to know. I saw the integrity in her separateness, and once she knew that, she tried as hard as she could to learn what she so deeply wanted to know.

Marie Clay talks of the crucial importance of observation in teaching children to read. When Rebekka knew she was seen, that I had indeed observed her, she learned how to learn.

When you teach a child to read, you don't make the difficulties in their life disappear. But you give them a chance in life.

For the teacher, there is a final part in teaching a child you have come to love, and that is letting go. The children don't need to depend on us. They need to understand their potential and use it. They need to see kindness and learn to repeat it themselves. With that we show them themselves and their relationship to the world.

On the first day of second grade, I pointed out Rebekka to a neighborhood mother I knew and said what a wonderful child she was, how much I enjoyed her. The mother looked at me a little surprised and said, "She looks so separate, so removed." I looked again at Rebekka, not through the closeness of knowing her well but trying to see her from a distance, and I saw what I had missed. There she was, standing appropriately in line, not moving, waiting patiently in her new school shoes, looking totally apart from everyone around. It was the first Rebekka I had known.

And there was good reason for her withdrawal. Jamaica had lost her lease three days before because the owner of her apartment was selling the building. She didn't know where she could go, she didn't know if her four kids could stay in the same school, and the fear of going back to an unsafe neighborhood or being out on the street had been bringing her far down. Things were hard, quiet, and uncertain at home. Rebekka didn't know if this school would be hers for long, and the safest thing was just to withdraw into herself again.

Jamaica did find a home. Rebekka stayed at Franklin and came to read to me often. But more important, her classroom teacher, a kind, warm soul, made Rebekka feel sure and seen. Six weeks after school started, I saw Rebekka walk into class with her arm around her teacher's waist, smiling. Rebekka knew she belonged, and she had given up her distance again.

Conclusion

I've now taught Reading Recovery for six years. It was in my first years as a Reading Recovery teacher that I taught Fortune, Nicholas, Kareem, Nkauj Hli, and Rebekka.

Kareem and Nkauj Hli are now in middle school. I've had sporadic contact with Kareem over the years. He's still the same kid he was in first grade, with the attitude now of a middle schooler. You still need his trust, and if you have it, Kareem will try to do his best. If you don't have it, he'll work hard at creating problems.

I went to see Kareem one day at the end of his fifth-grade year. He adored his fifth-grade teacher, a former University of Wisconsin football player, and stayed after school and came in before school to work with him. Kareem wanted to shine before him and did very well in fifth grade.

That day Kareem and I went to the school library, and I asked him to find some books to read to me. He went straight to the section on Native Americans, pulled down a book of poetry he was familiar with, and read it fluently. I was relieved (you're never quite sure you've succeeded) and impressed. We talked a bit, and then I said, "Read something else to me."

Kareem went right back to the same section and pulled out a book on Native American leaders. He brought it back to our table, and before reading it to me, he told me what it was about. He had been studying Native Americans with his teacher and had certain favorites. He read to me about Tecumseh and then a modern leader. Kareem not only could read but he could read to find out what he wanted to know, and he even had a favorite section of the library.

I saw him again—in the principal's office—when I visited his middle school this year. He is still in trouble regularly and has an attitude that precedes him. But fairness matters to Kareem, and if he thinks he's being treated fairly, he stays within certain bounds (although not necessarily the ones people would like). He still has tremendous kinetic energy—his body moving as he talks, his eyes looking intensely at what he's focused on—and as I talked with him, I thought about how difficult it must be to live inside a body with that energy.

Kareem was put in an emotionally disturbed pull-out program for middle school, over his fifth-grade teacher's objections, because of his social problems. He is mainstreamed, though, for all but that one class. His middle school has high standards and draws from some of the most highly educated neighborhoods in the city of Madison. Kareem is getting Bs and Cs there—this from a boy who didn't know what a tomato or lettuce was in first grade. I'm really proud of Kareem, and I'm certain Reading Recovery gave him that first necessary chance in school.

Nkauj Hli was given the Qualitative Reading Inventory at the end of fifth grade. She scored at the sixth-grade level for decoding and the fifth-grade level for comprehension. Now in middle school at the same very academic school as Kareem, she had over a B+ average last semester and was on the honor roll. Her teachers say she's a hard worker, and her younger sister said the same thing to me on the playground: "She's a good girl. She gets As and works hard." I saw her at an evening choir concert at her school, standing quiet and straight, still very shy, very dignified.

I know of two Madison schools Fortune has been in since she left Franklin in first grade, but each time that I heard she was at a school, her family moved before I could contact her. That means her family has moved at least four times in four years; I suspect the number of times is actually even higher.

Rebekka is the other one I worry about. Though she finished Reading Recovery right at grade level, she has fallen further behind each year. She finished fourth grade this year, and her teacher said she is now reading at about a third-grade level. She's had the best teachers, and each year the teachers have seen her grace, but something makes it difficult for her to learn. She's an abstract, reflective child who doesn't learn the way most kids do. She is one of those few kids who need close, individual help all through school. If she were from a well-to-do family, she would probably have tutors and make it. But her mother doesn't have the luxury of thinking about tutors for Rebekka. It's a loss to Rebekka and to us that we as a society are failing her.

Nicholas is doing well. He wrote to me when he was in third grade, thanking me for teaching him to read and enclosing a copy of a class newsletter to parents. In it his teacher wrote that Nicholas was the "class writer" and that students loved to stop and listen to the latest story Nicholas had written. Nicholas goes to middle school next year. His fifth-grade teacher saw him as a high-average student and said he read often. This year, like the other readers in his class, he went through the Goosebumps books one right after another.

After six years of teaching in Reading Recovery, I am still excited to start working with each new child, still excited to have the opportunity (which you don't have working with a group of even three children, let alone a whole class) to consider each of my Reading Recovery students so carefully each day that I will probably figure out why he or she is failing to learn to read. And I am still excited to give each child the gift of learning to read and becoming confident in their abilities.

First grade is an age of innocence and fanciful thinking when children actually *believe* that symbols represent something. They trust that the four letters *m, o, o,* and *n,* when put together in that order, really mean the moon in the sky. This abstraction requires a tremendous leap of faith—a willingness to accept that "this" is "that"—but one that is necessary to learn to read.

In thinking both about why most children do learn to read and about why learning and school are difficult for some, it can be helpful to go back and think about a time when learning was hard for us.

In school, I always dreaded science and the specificity of it. I could memorize vocabulary in foreign languages easily because the words held meaning for me. I loved thinking about how similar and different the words were; how Latin had been recast into French, Spanish, and English because of people, space, and time. I believed in the importance of what

I was learning because it was magical to me. Analogy, how this word in French meant that word in English, held history and story and transformation all at once. (Clearly, people who love science see the excitement of transformation, meaning, and analogy in it that I see in language.)

But I dreaded chemistry and biology because they didn't hold that sense of ambiguity and unexpected change that language did for me. In French, there was the possibility of learning many words to represent one thing, and a single word itself could mean more than one thing. Two words could mean almost the same thing, but might not, depending on the situation. All this amazed me then, and still does.

Chemistry and biology were based on the sureness and importance of one thing having one name; of each experiment leading to only one correct result. Because as a high school student I didn't believe in the importance of seeing the world this way, I didn't believe in the system of representation in science. And so there was no magic for me in learning it.

Six-year-olds still haven't put borders on what is real and what is imaginary. For them, believing something and believing *in* something, trusting it, are much the same thing. Most six-year-olds willingly believe the magic of what they learn. And with this belief they learn an entire system of visual representation—they learn to read.

We rarely ask older children or adults to construct understanding at the level of abstraction and coherence that we ask of six-year-olds in learning to read. Reading is an amazing, complex skill. Yet most children do learn to read without much difficulty.

But young children who have problems with reading generally become older children and then adults who have problems with reading. And then, as they continue to try to learn to read, they have an added difficulty: reading becomes something they no longer believe they can understand. They are *too* aware of the relationship between the symbol and what it represents—they know now that "this" really *isn't* "that"— and so proceed in reading slowly, doubting all the time that they have unlocked the key.

If only for this reason—that young children are still willing to believe that reading is real—it is crucial to catch struggling children early, before they have learned to fail, and teach them that they can read. Now is when they can learn. If we try to teach them later, they make progress but rarely catch up to their peers.

There is a social reason for investing in teaching all of our children to read well—so that our society is literate and has the skills to maintain democracy.

There is also an individual, one-child-at-a-time reason for it, and that is to keep children like Nicholas and Nkauj Hli from being so sadly disappointed in themselves. It is to try to give Rebekka a sense of the beauty of her soul and its connection to words and school. It is to give Fortune something to hold on to in life as her parents keep her in a whirlwind. It is to give Kareem a solid chance at not being the bad boy who drops out of school.

These were just five kids. There are thousands and thousands more.

Bibliography

The following is a list of books on Reading Recovery and books that have influenced my teaching of children.

Ashton-Warner, Sylvia. *Teacher.* New York: Simon and Schuster, 1963.

Clay, Marie. *Becoming Literate: The Construction of Inner Control.* Portsmouth, N.H.: Heinemann, 1991.

———. *The Early Detection of Reading Difficulties.* Portsmouth, N.H.: Heinemann, 1993.

———. *An Observation Survey of Early Literacy Achievement.* Portsmouth, N. H.: Heinemann, 1993.

———. *Reading Recovery: A Guidebook for Teachers in Training.* Portsmouth, N. H.: Heinemann, 1993.

Comer, James P. *Maggie's American Dream.* New York: Penguin, 1988.

Cowley, Joy. *Whole Learning, Whole Child.* Bothell, Wash.: Wright Group, 1993.

DeFord, Diane E., Carol A. Lyons, and Gay Su Pinnell. *Bridges to Literacy: Learning from Reading Recovery.* Portsmouth, N. H.: Heinemann, 1991.

Eco, Umberto. *A Theory of Semiotics.* Bloomington: University of Indiana Press, 1976.

Escamilla, Kathy, Ana María Andrade, Amelia G. M. Basurto, and Olivia A. Ruiz in collaboration with Marie M. Clay. *Instrumento de observación de los logros de la lecto-escritura inicial: Spanish Reconstruction of An Observation Survey, a Bilingual Text.* Portsmouth, N. H.: Heinemann, 1996.

Graves, Donald. *Writing: Teachers and Children at Work.* Portsmouth, N. H.: Heinemann, 1983.

Johnson, Katie. *Doing Words.* Boston: Houghton Mifflin, 1987.

Markova, Dawna. *How Your Child Is Smart.* Berkeley: Conari Press, 1992.

Thích, Nhât Hanh. *Interbeing.* Berkeley: Parallax Press, 1993.

———. *The Miracle of Mindfulness.* Boston: Beacon Press, 1976.

For further information on Reading Recovery®:

The Reading Recovery Council of North America
1929 Kenny Road, Suite 100
Columbus, OH 43210-1069
Tel: (614) 292-7111
Fax: (614) 292-4404